TRANSITION PLANNING FOR STUDENTS WITH DISABILITIES

ABOUT THE AUTHORS

Jeffrey P. Bakken, Ph.D., is Professor and Chair, Department of Special Education at Illinois State University. He has a Bachelor's Degree in Elementary Education from the University of Wisconsin–LaCrosse, and graduate degrees in the area of Special Education-Learning Disabilities from Purdue University. Dr. Bakken is a teacher, consultant, and scholar. His specific areas of interest include transition, teacher effectiveness, assessment, learning strategies, and technology. He has written more than 75 academic publications, including journal articles, chapters, monographs, reports, and proceedings; and he has made over 180 presentations at local, state, regional, national, and international levels. Dr. Bakken has received the College of Education and the University Research Initiative Award, the College of Education Outstanding College Researcher Award, the College of Education Outstanding College Teacher Award, and the Outstanding University Teacher Award from Illinois State University. Additionally, he is on the editorial boards of many scholarly publications, including *Multicultural Learning and Teaching, Remedial and Special Education,* and *Multiple Voices.* Through his work, he has committed himself toward improving teachers' knowledge and techniques as well as services for students with exceptionalities and their families.

Festus E. Obiakor, Ph.D., is Professor and Coordinator of Graduate Programs, Department of Exceptional Education at the University of Wisconsin-Milwaukee. His graduate degrees are from Texas Christian University and New Mexico State University. Dr. Obiakor is a teacher, scholar, and consultant. His specific areas of interests include self-concept development, multicultural psychology and special education, comparative/international education, and educational reform/program evaluation. Dr. Obiakor has written more than 150 academic publications including books, chapters, articles, and commentaries. He has served as Distinguished Visiting Professor/Scholar at Frostburg State University, Hendrix College, Indiana University of Pennsylvania, Portland State University, the University of Georgia, Eastern Illinois University, Marquette University, West Virginia University, Hampton University, Illinois State University, Brigham Young University, Tennessee State University, Morgan State University, Grambling State University, and Indiana-Purdue University. Additionally, Dr. Obiakor is on the editorial boards of many scholarly publications, including *Multicultural Learning and Teaching,* and *Multiple Voices,* in which he currently serves as co-executive editor and co-editor, respectively. In his teachings, writings, workshops, and presentations, he has continued to prescribe multidimensional methods of assessment, divergent teaching techniques, and a comprehensive support model to connect the self, the family, the school, and the community in providing learning opportunities and choices for *all* students.

TRANSITION PLANNING FOR STUDENTS WITH DISABILITIES

What Educators and Service Providers Can Do

By

JEFFREY P. BAKKEN, Ph.D.

Illinois State University

and

FESTUS E. OBIAKOR, Ph.D.

University of Wisconsin at Milwaukee

CHARLES C THOMAS • PUBLISHER, LTD.
Springfield • Illinois • U.S.A.

Published and Distributed Throughout the World by

CHARLES C THOMAS • PUBLISHER, LTD.
2600 South First Street
Springfield, Illinois 62704

©2008 by CHARLES C THOMAS • PUBLISHER, LTD.

ISBN 978-0-398-07788-4 (hard)
ISBN 978-0-398-07789-1 (paper)

Library of Congress Catalog Card Number: 2007034975

With THOMAS BOOKS *careful attention is given to all details of man-
ufacturing and design. It is the Publisher's desire to present books that are satisfactory as to their physical qualities and artistic possibilities and appropriate for their particular use.* THOMAS BOOKS *will be true to those laws
of quality that assure a good name and good will.*

Printed in the United States of America
CR-R-3

Library of Congress Cataloging-in-Publication Data

Bakken, Jeffrey P.
 Transition planning for students with disabilities : what educators
and service providers can do / by Jeffrey P. Bakken and Festus E.
Obiakor.
  p. cm.
 Includes bibliographical references and index.
 ISBN 978-0-398-07788-4 (hard) -- ISBN 978-0-398-07789-1 (pbk.)
 1. Youth with disabilities--Education--United States. 2. School-to-
work transition--United States. 3. Students with disabilities--Services
for--United States. I. Obiakor, Festus E. II. Title.

LC4031.B35 2007
371.9'043--dc22

                                          2007034975

To my wife, Heidi, and children, Jared and Emma. Your encouragement, love, patience, and support have helped me to maximize my potential as a teacher, scholar, professional, and leader.

To my wife, Pauline, and children, Charles, Gina, Kristen, and Alicia. I cannot imagine where I would be today as a teacher, scholar, professional, and leader without your patience, love, and support.

FOREWORD

In the *Merriam-Webster's Online Dictionary* (2005), transition is defined as a "passage from one state, stage, subject, or place to another; a movement, development, or evolution from one form, stage, or style to another; a musical modulation; a musical passage leading from one section of a piece to another; and an abrupt change in energy state or level (as of an atomic nucleus or a molecule) usually accompanied by loss or gain of a single quantum of energy." Clearly, these definitions, as different as they may seem, touch on some form of stage-by-stage movement, change, or advancement. A logical extension is that transition from school to adult life for students with disabilities represents a passage from one stage in life to the next or represents an abrupt change, despite the planning that might be provided as they move from a mandated system of *programs* to a system of services based on eligibility. It is common knowledge that leaving high school can be a critical point in everyone's life! It is a time when important decisions are made that will impact the rest of a young adult's life creating the intricate possibilities for postsecondary education, career development, and relationship building with people outside the school system. Put another way, the transition period can definitely be rewarding, hectic, and challenging for a young adult or anyone for that matter.

In writing the Foreword of this book, I began to think about my own transition from school to adult life. While it was almost 30 years ago, the memories still remain vivid! As with many of us, I had *good* teachers and *not-so-good* teachers. It was the *not-so-good* teachers who tried to negatively influence my high school career. I still remember the chemistry teacher who told us that if we did not understand a particular concept, that eventually the "gods" would come down and bestow knowledge on us. In addition, I remember the geometry teacher who told us that "some day the light bulb would go on." Instead of engaging me in the experience of learning for my future, these teachers, inadvertently, tried to kill my spirit by suggesting that I just was not smart enough –because the gods never came down and the light bulb never did go on. Needless to say, being a class clown was much more comfortable for me at that point. When the time came for high school graduation and all my friends were meeting with the school counselor to apply for college, I did the same. I met with this counselor only to be told that I was "not college material and should just get married and have a family." While I do not see anything wrong with getting married and having a family, it was not motivating to hear such statements. I never forgot those statements that could have negatively impacted my future had I let them. Instead, I chose my own path! I found a way to get into college on my own; and graduate with degrees! Today, I am a college professor. Like many students, my future could have been determined by that school counselor, that chemistry teacher, and that geometry teacher. Maybe, it was my naiveté or stubbornness; but I believed the only challenge I had were the limitations I put on myself. But, not every student is that fortunate to have that kind of resiliency and self-determination. More often than not, I remember my own experiences when I work with young adults during their final years of high school as we prepare and plan for their future.

Realizing successful postschool outcomes for students with disabilities is a goal we all strive for as educators and service providers. In *Transition Planning for Students with Disabilities: What Educators and Service Providers Can Do*, Dr. Jeffrey P. Bakken and Dr. Festus E. Obiakor provide an expansive discussion about each area of transition impacting the lives of students with disabilities. Consider the wonderfully organized chapters and themes of the book. Chapters 1 and 2 provide the reader with a foundation of transition services and a historical overview of models and practices; Chapter 3 offers a critical look at transition with students from culturally and ethnically diverse backgrounds; Chapter 4 presents an in-depth look at assistive technology to assist students in fully participating in the planning for their future beyond high school; Chapters 5 and 6 describe the process for planning and the importance of family collaboration; Chapters 7, 8, and 9 discuss career development and the importance of work experiences; Chapters 9 and 10 provide a review of social skills and leisure options; Chapter 11 looks at independent living options and the fundamental skills needed for living independently; and Chapter 12 identifies successful postsecondary education programs.

While transition services have been mandated by the Individuals with Disabilities Act (IDEA) since 1990, bridging the gap between school and adult services continues to be a challenge for all stakeholders. In this book, Bakken and Obiakor discuss bridge-building ideas through the collaboration, consultation, and cooperation of all. This book is written for today's researchers, scholars, and practitioners. No doubt, educators, service providers, related professionals, and parents will find it useful as they work together to enhance postschool outcomes for young adults with disabilities.

Laura Owens, Ph.D.
University of Wisconsin–Milwaukee

REFERENCE

Merriam-Webster's Online Dictionary. (2005). Springfield, MA: Merriam-Webster Inc. http://www.m-w.com/.

PREFACE

The need for transition services for students with exceptionalities is apparent and critical for their success after high school. While still in school, general and special education teachers, parents, students, administrators, and other service providers need to provide the proper assessment, instruction, and guidance for these students to be successful. *Transition Planning for Students with Disabilities: What Educators and Service Providers Can Do* is an important book that focuses on all aspects of transition planning from school to postschool levels. We believe it is essential for school professionals, parents, and students to work collaboratively and consultively to determine each student's future goals and develop an effective plan to meet those goals successfully.

Transition Planning for Students with Disabilities discusses critical transition topics for this day and age. In this book, Chapter 1 discusses "Transitioning Students with Disabilities: Preparing for Life;" Chapter 2 focuses on "Transition Models and Practices;" Chapter 3 addresses "Transition and Culturally and Linguistically Diverse Learners;" Chapter 4 explains "Selecting Appropriate Assistive Technology for Student Transition;" Chapter 5 provides information on "Planning and Developing Student-focused Individualized Transition Plans;" Chapter 6 explores "Collaborating with Families in the Transition Process;" Chapter 7 discusses "Job and Career Development: Understanding the Nature and Types of Jobs;" Chapter 8 focuses on "Employment Training, Support, and Vocational/Technical Education;" Chapter 9 addresses "Social Outcomes and Community Resources;" Chapter 10 provides information on "Transportation Education and Leisure/ Recreation Outcomes;" Chapter 11 explains "Independent Living Outcomes, Residential Opportunities, Group Homes and Intermediate Care;" and finally, Chapter 12 discusses "Post-Secondary Education Outcomes." Each chapter describes a part of the transition plan-

Transition Planning for Students with Disabilities

ning process, as well as offers suggestions for effective planning and additional resources that can be useful when working with individuals with exceptionalities.

Although the content of this book addresses topics that are commonly found in other books, the format and other aspects are unique. The text is written in a style that all readers can comprehend and understand; and the information can be easily applied to classroom and transition programs. In this book, we wanted to explain a comprehensive structure of transition programming using real cases to captivate the reader's attention. Put another way, we wanted to provide the rationale for transition programming in schools. On the whole, this book will be an excellent resource to researchers, scholars, educators, and service providers. We are confident that its readers will find it helpful and useful in their efforts to transition students with exceptionalities into a world of work. Hopefully, this book will be a required or supplementary text for undergraduate and graduate transition courses in special education.

This book would not have been possible without the support of family, friends, and colleagues. We thoroughly appreciate every feedback that we received. Finally, we thank Dr. Laura Owens of the University of Wisconsin–Milwaukee for writing the Foreword of this book.

J. P. B.
F. E. O.

CONTENTS

TRANSITION PLANNING FOR STUDENTS WITH DISABILITIES

Chapter 1

TRANSITIONING STUDENTS WITH DISABILITIES: PREPARING FOR LIFE

Joe is a sophomore in high school and beginning to think about what he would like to do after graduation. Joe has a learning disability and has some difficulties with reading comprehension and written expression, but is very strong in mathematics and has very good communication skills. It will be important to consider Joe's abilities when developing his transition plan. His parents are very involved with his schooling and want what's best for him after high school, given his abilities. His case manager, Mr. Johnson, understands how critical transition is to positive outcomes after graduation and wants to get Joe and his parents involved in the transition process as soon as possible. Mr. Johnson realizes it is important to work with Joe and his parents and get their input on a transition plan to help prepare Joe for life after high school.

What happens to students like Joe above when their parents are unaware of the possibilities of different transition services as well as the transition process? This chapter answers this critical question. Students are involved with many transitions throughout their educational careers, such as moving from elementary school to junior high or from junior high to high school. These transitions are important in the students' lives; however, the transition from the secondary level to postsecondary education or the world of work is the most critical for all students, especially those with disabilities. The preparation for this transition begins early in a student's life and continues throughout his or her educational career and beyond. This transition from school to work is essential to ensure positive postschool outcomes for students with disabilities. "Transition and person-centered planning approaches can improve outcomes by making education more relevant, by giving students more control over their lives, and by focusing on goals important to them (Flexer, Simmons, Luft, & Baer, 2005, p. 9). Research (Blackorby & Wagner, 1996) involving the post-school outcomes for students with disabilities sheds light on the fact that their outcomes were less successful than their peers without disabilities. The federal requirements for transition services grew out of a perceived need based on this research regarding postschool outcomes of students with disabilities.

Findings from the National Longitudinal Transition Study have shown that, compared to students without disabilities, students with disabilities had lower rates of competitive employment, residential independence, and postsecondary degrees (Blackorby & Wagner, 1996). In addition, the study found that school factors contributed significantly to postschool outcomes of students with disabilities. For example, students who had vocational education and work experience in high school had a higher probability of finding competitive employment after high school. The findings also showed that "postschool paths of youth with disabilities reflected their transition goals" (NLTS, 1993, p. 16). This finding supports the fact that transition planning is critical to ensuring positive outcomes for students with disabilities after graduation. As a result of the National Longitudinal Transition Study, as well as other research involving postschool outcomes and quality-of-life of students with disabilities, federal legislation has required that Individualized Education Programs include statements of transition service needs for students ages 16 and older (IDEIA, 2004). This focus on transition planning and services has led to more research in best practices in the field of transition to improve students' life activities after school.

TRANSITION SERVICES: CONCEPTUALIZATIONS AND MEANINGS

Transition can be defined as moving from one place to another. With regards to students, especially students with disabilities, the meaning of the word *transition* is much more focused. This type of transition is the movement from secondary school to postsecondary education, work, and community involvement. *Transition services*, then, are the vehicles that help to ensure that each student with a disability makes that important step as successfully as possible. According to the Individuals with Disabilities Education Improvement Act (IDEIA 2004), transition services are defined as "a coordinated set of activities for a child with a disability that (a) is designed to be within a results-oriented process, that is focused on improving the academic and functional achievement of the child with a disability to facilitate the child's movement from school to postschool activities, including postsecondary education, vocational education, integrated employment (including supported employment), continuing and adult education, adult services, independent living, or community participation; (b) is based on the individual child's needs, taking into account the child's strengths, preferences, and interests; and (c) includes instruction, related services, community experiences, the development of employment and other postschool adult living objectives, and, when appropriate, acquisition of daily living skills and functional vocational evaluation." Some of the important aspects of the federal definition are that transition services need to be coordinated and results-oriented for each student with a disability. In addition, these services must be individualized to each student's strengths and interests, and not just a "checklist" of typical transition-related activities and skills (McAfee & Greenawalt, 2001). Finally, the federal definition also includes the integration of a variety of service delivery types (i.e., direct instruction, work programs, and community experiences) and the involvement of agencies (i.e., independent living, supported employment, and Medicaid) that can assist the student after graduation.

The goal of transition services is to assist students with disabilities to achieve their career and life goals, as well as become active members of their communities. The goal, then, of the Individualized Education Plan (IEP) team should be to effectively and accurately evaluate the students' strengths, interests, preferences, and needs, and create a plan that successfully addresses and incorporates as many of these as possible. In doing this, the IEP teams can help to ensure that students with disabilities are productive workers and members of their communities. As it appears, the legal mandates for transition in IDEIA 2004 have expanded the transition requirements laid out in IDEA 1997. According to IDEIA 2004, a transition plan must be incorporated into a student's IEP "beginning not later than the first IEP to be in effect when the child is 16, and updated annually thereafter." The plan must include "appropriate measurable postsecondary goals based upon age appropriate transition assessments related to training, education, employment, and, where appropriate, independent living skills, [and] the transition services (including courses of study) needed to assist the child in reaching those goals." These requirements focus more on the need for postsecondary goals that are based on data from various assessments of the student's strengths and needs. This data must drive the creation of appropriate goals for each student that must, in turn, be measurable so that the IEP team can determine the student's progress toward each goal. IDEIA requirements continue to involve the use of a variety of service delivery styles and linkages to other agencies that can benefit the student after graduation. Additionally, these requirements include reporting students' progress toward all IEP goals to parents, and postsecondary goals concurrent with their report cards. Parents and students must be informed of their rights. In other words, when a student reaches 17 years old, he/she and his/her parents must be informed that at age 18 rights to special education will transfer to the student alone. For some students with severe and multiple disabilities, this provision may not be applicable. However, for most students with disabilities this transfer of rights must be clearly explained to both the student and his/her parents, to ensure understanding of the law.

TRANSITION SERVICES PLANNING

IDEIA 2004 sets out the legal mandates for what must be included in the IEP of each student with a disability as they relate to transition services and when those services must begin. However, the process of transition planning is much more complex than the brief statement in the law. Many different factors come into play and should be examined while planning for successful transitions. All of these factors may not be applicable for all students, but they should at least be considered when developing a student's transition plan. First, the diversity among students with disabilities makes it necessary for IEP teams to be culturally sensitive and aware of individual differences and values when planning for transition. These differences may be related to culture, language, or family background. Collaborating with families is essential to understanding the background and goals of the student, as well as involving the family as part of IEP and transition plans. Another overarching factor that needs to be considered in transition planning is assistive technology. IDEIA 2004 also requires IEP teams to consider assistive technology needs for students with disabilities. Even though the use of assistive technology likely begins earlier in a student's educational career, his needs for assistive technology do not end upon graduation and must also be included in the development of his or her postsecondary goals.

IDEIA 2004 requires that transition services be individualized to the strengths and needs of each student. In order to achieve that end, transition planning should be student-focused with the student direct-ly involved in the discussions and decision-making (Kohler & Field, 2003). This helps students to develop and increase self-determination skills by allowing them to make choices and advocate for themselves. The IEP team should not be making decisions for students, but rather collaborating with them to determine the most appropriate goals and services for them. For many students with disabilities, some type of postsecondary education will be a part of their transition plan. This could be within a vocational/technical program, a community college, or a four-year college or university. For the IEP team, this means that the student will need to be prepared for both admission to and partic-ipation in that postsecondary education program. In addition, the team must (a) work with the student in determining his/her career goals, (b) help him/her to find an appropriate program, and (c) moti-vate him/her to learn and practice the job skills necessary for the cho-sen career. Apparently, there are many aspects to career and job development that the IEP team should address during transition plan-ning. Assessment of the student's job skills and interests is of vital importance in developing appropriate postsecondary goals for that student. For instance, for some students, it is necessary to create link-ages to agencies that can work with them after graduation, such as in supported employment settings. The education and skills training that a student receives related to job and career development is an invalu-able component of the transition plan.

In conjunction with a student's preparation for the workforce, the IEP team must assess other aspects of independent living for the stu-dent. For example, the team should examine the student's social skills, independent living skills, ability to find and utilize appropriate trans-portation, and ability to seek out and participate in recreation and leisure activities. For some students, there may not be a need for post-secondary goals in these areas; however, other students may need training and community experiences to increase their skills. These areas are critical in order for students to be active members of their communities, as well as to have a better quality of life. Clearly, all aspects of transition planning can enhance the process, but they can also make the process more complicated. For example, to enhance transition planning, there must be good record keeping. Organizing and maintaining good records are helpful to the IEP team during the planning and delivery of transition services, and invaluable to students and their parents for use after graduation. Since assessment for transition needs can take many forms, such as observations, interest inventories, and various job skill assessments, it is essential for data and corresponding records to be accurate and organized. In addition, having good records can make the development of appropriate postsecondary goals much easier. On the whole, it is important for IEP teams to have a plan for collecting and maintaining transition-related data and records (e.g., who will be responsible for maintaining and updating the records, and how the records will be organized). There are different types of forms that have been created to help IEP teams keep important transition-related information updated and organized for ease of use (e.g., Neubert & Moon, 2000; Ohio Valley Educational Cooperative, 1996). The amount of recordkeeping necessary for a student will depend on the complexity of his/her needs. According to Pierangelo and Giuliani (2004), record keeping should include official documents (e.g., high school transcripts, medical records, teacher reports, IEPs and evaluations, work program or job training reports, interest inventories, and letters of recommendation). As they indicated, other information to be kept should include parent letters, meeting summaries, organization brochures, and agency contracts.

FINAL THOUGHTS

This chapter has addressed the need for transition services for students with disabilities, based on research involving postschool outcomes for these students. The legal definition of and requirements for transition services are highlighted and explained. It is essential for school professionals, parents, and students to work collaboratively to determine each student's future goals and develop an effective plan to meet those goals successfully. This chapter (and other chapters in this book) give individuals involved with the transition of exceptional learners a resource for transition planning and service delivery that is understandable and addresses all aspects of effective transition services. Topics such as assistive technology, families, employment training and support, leisure activities, and independent living are just some of the important issues that will be discussed in this book. Each chapter describes a part of the transition planning process, as well as offer suggestions for effective planning and additional resources that can be useful for these individuals.

Chapter 2

TRANSITION MODELS AND PRACTICES

Maria is 15 years old and is a freshman in high school. She has an educational diagnosis of a developmental disability, with an intelligence quotient (IQ) of 65, and difficulties in reading, mathematics, written expression, social skills, organizational skills, and adaptive behavior. She reads at the second grade level but has pretty good auditory comprehension skills. She is working on improving her basic facts, telling time, and money skills in math. In writing, she can write her name, address, and other personal information as well as simple sentences containing simple ideas. In a one-on-one situation, Maria functions very well, but in groups, she sometimes loses her focus and behaves inappropriately. Maria's parents are very supportive and communicate regularly with her teachers and case manager and Maria is also learning to advocate effectively for herself. After high school, Maria's parents would like her to live and function independently, if possible. For instance, they would like her to hold a job, live in a group home or apartment, and function adequately in the community (i.e., use transportation and engage in leisure activities). As it appears, Maria is interested in living away from her home and holding a job. Currently, she likes plants and animals and those might be two areas to investigate for possible future career choices.

Based on the above case, it is important to ask, what type of transition model and practices could help Maria to be successful in high school, be prepared for her future career, and function independently in the community? This chapter responds to this critical question. If we look back in history, we will find that transition services for youth with disabilities began as early as in the 1930s for deaf students and in the 1940s for students with mental retardation (Rusch, Szymanski, &

Chadsey-Rusch, 1992). Transition services have been around for more than 80 years but have really only been mandated in the last 20 years for students with disabilities. What are transition services and what does transition mean? In its most basic context, the term transition means change or "passage from one place, condition, or action to another" (Funk & Wagnalls New International Dictionary of the English Language, 1995, p. 1334). In special education, transition is used to describe a systematic passage from school to adult life for students with disabilities. According to the Individuals with Disabilities Education Improvement Act (IDEIA, 2004), transition is designed to be within a results-oriented process that is focused on improving the academic and functional achievement of the child with a disability to facilitate his or her movement from school to postschool activities, including postsecondary education, vocational education, integrated employment (including supported employment), continuing and adult education, adult services, independent living, or community participation.

The historical roots of transition can be found in both programmatic and legal/regulatory efforts. Halpern (1992) traced the conceptual and philosophical roots of the transition movement to the 1960s with the early work-study program. The goal was ". . . to create an integrated academic, social, and vocational curriculum, accompanied by appropriate work experience, that was designed to prepare students with mild disabilities for eventual community adjustment" (p. 203). Halpern added that most of these programs died in the 1970s due to a variety of problems related to funding, certification, supervision, and the "similar benefits" sections of new legislation (i.e., 1973 amendments to the Rehabilitation Act and Public Law 94–142) that altered roles and responsibilities of public agencies.

The passage and subsequent implementation of the Americans with Disabilities Act (ADA) of 1990 raised expectations for further improvement in the employment of persons with disabilities during this decade. However, Trupin, Sebesta, Yelin, and LaPlante (1997) established that the enforcement mechanisms of the ADA had not yet proved sufficient to begin closing the gap in employment rates between persons with and without disabilities. Around the same period, the School-to-Work Opportunities Act was developed in 1994. This Act is a national framework within which all states would create statewide systems. This law called for major restructuring and significant systemic changes to facilitate the creation of a universal, high-quality, school-to-work system that will enable all students to successfully enter the workforce. All students are defined to include individuals with disabilities. Apparently, this law contained three major components: school-based learning, work-based learning, and connecting activities.

Before the School-to-Work Opportunities Act was developed, the government initiated the Individuals with Disabilities Education Act (IDEA, 1990) later amended in 1997 as IDEA 1997 and identified three primary transitional stages in the educational lives of children with disabilities: (a) early intervention to preschool, (b) preschool to elementary school, and (c) secondary school to adult life (Section 674(b)(3)(C)(i-iii)). The 1997 amendments to IDEA reflect the influence of standards-based reform and, like other educational legislation during the mid-1990s, the reauthorized IDEA focused on student outcomes. IDEA's transition planning requirements lowered the age of identification of students' transition needs to age 14 and the development and implementation of a transition plan for all students with disabilities starting at the age of 16 (or younger, when deemed appropriate). The IDEA provisions require a statement of needed transition services be included in the individualized education program (IEP) for each student beginning no later than age 16, and at a younger age if determined appropriate. Additionally, these provisions require that the services be updated on an annual basis. In 2004, IDEA was reauthorized as the Individuals with Disabilities Improvement Act (IDEIA). IDEIA updated transition stipulations stating that services should begin not later than the first IEP to be in effect when the child is 16, and updated annually thereafter (Section 602(34)(A). Also, appropriate measurable postsecondary goals based upon age appropriate transition assessments related to training, education, employment, and, where appropriate, independent living skills need to be developed. In addition, transition services (including courses of study) need to assist the child in reaching these goals (Section 614(d)(1)(A)(VIII)(aa)(bb).

One of the more challenging initiatives of the 1990s for the field of special education was the standards-based reform movement, which began with education reforms in the 1980s and became more focused with passage of Goals 2000: Educate America Act and the Improving America's Schools Act (the reauthorized Elementary and Secondary

Education Act) in 1994. When initially authorized, the U.S. Department of Education viewed the School-to-Work Opportunities Act as an essential component of standards-based reform as promoted by Goals 2000 (Riley, 1995). The School-to-Work Opportunities Act was enacted to complement Goals 2000 by ensuring that students learn relevant workplace skills and have relevant work experiences (Smith & Scoll, 1995). All of these focused on transition of students from a school to work environment. The ultimate goal was to enable young people to assume these rights and responsibilities so they can function and contribute in the adult world as independently as possible.

DIFFERENT TRANSITION MODELS

Transition services can be traced back to the 1930s and 1940s, but not until the 1960s were educational and vocational models developed to comprehensively address the dimensions of adult adjustment. Early efforts included (a) cooperative work-study programs, (b) Career Education Movement, (c) OSERS "Bridge" Model of Transition, (d) Halpern's Revised Model of Transition, (e) the Experience Based Model, (f) the Home/Community Based Model, (g) the Rural Residential Model, (h) the School-Based Comprehensive Career Education Model, (i) the School-Based Comprehensive Career Education Model, and (j) Commencement programs. These mandatory transition services foreshadowed the development of an integrated academic, social, and vocational curriculum in conjunction with work experience (Halpern, 1992).

Cooperative Work Study Programs

Cooperative work study programs for students with mild disabilities could be considered a precursor to the present models of transition (see Halpern, 1992). Work study programs were conducted cooperatively between public schools and local offices of vocational rehabilitation through formal agreements. Teachers spent half of their time as work study coordinators supervising students in community work placements and the other half of their time as classroom teachers.

Career Education Movement

The career education movement began in the 1970s. The concept of career education was first introduced in 1971 by the U.S. Commissioner of Education at the national conference for secondary school principals (Marland, 1971). Unlike work study programs, career education was more general in focus and implementation. Early career education programs did not address the inclusion of students with disabilities. With increased federal attention and funding during the 1970s, the career education movement broadened to include students with disabilities (Issacson & Brown, 1993). This movement focused exclusively on the transition of students with disabilities from school to employment.

OSERS "Bridge" Model of Transition

Will (1984) noted that the Office of Special Education and Rehabilitation Services (OSERS) defined transition as "a bridge between the security and structure offered by the school to work and adult life requires sound preparation in the secondary school, adequate support at the point of school leaving, and secure opportunities and services, if needed, in adult situations" (p. 2). The model focused on secondary special education, vocational education, and other school-based services providing the foundation of skills, attitudes, personal relationships, and employer contacts that impact future success. The model is based upon three types of services offered to students with disabilities upon exit from public school programs, namely: (a) transition without special services for students with disabilities who make the transition by relying on their own resources or those generic services available to all students; (b) transition with time-limited services for students with disabilities seeking specialized short-term services to secure employment (e.g., vocational rehabilitation services); and (c) transition with ongoing services for students with severe disabilities who need ongoing support to sustain employment. Unlike the first two methods of transition, this third bridge required major changes to policies and programs because of the unavailability of these services during the early 1980s (Morningstar, Kleinhammer-Tramill, & Lattin, 1999).

Halpern's Revised Model of Transition

In 1985, Andrew Halpern expanded the OSERS Bridge Model beyond transition from school to employment. His revised model suggested that transition programs should be geared toward living successfully in the community (i.e., community adjustment). Halpern's emphasis on the outcome of community adjustment required that schools add to the Bridge Model the quality of residential environments as well as the importance of social and interpersonal networks (Morningstar et al., 1999).

The Experience-Based Model (EBCE)

At first labeled the Employer-Based model, EBCE offers an alternative system of secondary education to youths from 13 to 18 years old. The EBCE model is distinguished from traditional work/study programs on the basis that the program does not emphasize vocational skills, that it is an unpaid experience, that it includes career exploration and employer-site rotation procedures, that it uses experiential education for conveying learning in academic areas, that it allows a greater student role in shaping an personalized educational plan and, lastly, that it is not targeted to dropouts, disadvantaged, or other specific populations (Gardner & Warren, 1978). The EBCE Model for students with special needs (Larson, 1981) was based on the original Appalachia Education Laboratory Model (Goldhammer & Taylor, 1972) for students in general education. The program emphasized the opportunity for students to explore possible jobs while still enrolled in school. This makes it necessary for the business community to be an extension of the school. Logically, the program can be success only if effective coordination between them occurs. During a student's secondary program, four different job sites can generally be explored. Since the students work for no pay, their evaluation of what kind of work they prefer is unbiased by the money they earn. This allows them to make a more objective choice of full-time employment at the completion of the program.

The Home/Community-Based Model

The Home/Community Based model was originally conceptualized to be a system for providing educational services to the home. In addition, it focused on providing career counseling services by telephone for adults using a paraprofessional system (Gardner & Warren, 1978). Today, in some circles, it operates with a Resource Center which contains career-related materials for and about adults. The goal has been to provide services at home to help transition people with disabilities to where they need to be.

Rural Residential Model

This model focuses on providing services for chronically underemployed, multi-problem rural families. It offers training, remedial education, guidance for children, career counseling, and job placement for entire families with the goal of making the family unit economically viable. Heads of households are expected to participate a minimum of 40 hours per week in the program and spouses may participate 20–40 hours per week. Program areas include home management; health education; counseling; career guidance; and foundational educational and occupational preparations in carpentry, plumbing, electrical, air conditioning, lodging and food services, transportation, office education, marketing and distribution (Gardner & Warren, 1978).

The School-Based Comprehensive Career Education Model (CCEM)

In the School-Based Comprehensive Career Education Model practitioners have generally utilized a four or five stage model with some stages overlapping one another. Stage 1 is usually referred to as the *Career Awareness Stage.* No attempt to "train" occurs in this stage. In this model, students are expected to develop awareness of many careers available, awareness of self in relation to careers, respect and appreciation for all works in all fields, and to make tentative choices of career clusters to explore in mid-school years. Stage 2 is commonly referred to as the *Career Exploration Stage.* This stage begins around grade 5 or 6 and extends into the middle school or junior high school. Students' objectives include exploration of key occupational areas, assessment of career interests and abilities, development of awareness of relevant decision-making factors, gaining experience in meaningful decision making, development of tentative occupational plans, and arrival at tentative career choices. Students explore the world of work and receive "hands-on" experiences. Stage 3 is generally called the *Career Preparation Stage*. This occurs for students at approximately grades 9–12. The major goal is for students to develop either entry level job skills or be prepared for advanced occupational training. Stage 4 is called the *Career Specialization Stage*. Portions of this state are sometimes combined with portions of Stage 3. Many models also include an *Adult and Continuing Education Stage* (a possible Stage V) in this stage. The concentration here is on advanced career preparation above the high school level. It includes apprenticeships, associate degree programs, vocational certificate programs, and undergraduate and advanced degree programs (see Gardner & Warren, 1978).

While this was not specifically developed to help students with disabilities, its elements allow for the inclusion of people with disabilities since it provides ample opportunities for accommodating their unique needs. This is a three-dimensional model that contains four distinct path-ways to successful transition beyond school for youths with disabilities. Clearly, this model (a) is applicable to individuals with a broad range of disabilities, (b) offers course-of-study specifications for youths age 14 who have disabilities, (c) contains IDEA 1997 IEP transition language requirements for youths age 16 who have disabilities, and (d) outlines transient programming components for each pathway. In Pathway 1, a fully integrated high school college preparatory curriculum leading to passing of district proficiency exams, graduation requirements, and application requirements for entrance into a four-year university is implemented. In Pathway 2, a semi-integrated high school curriculum leading to passing of district proficiency exams, graduation requirements, and all requirements for entrance into a community college or professional vocational school is the focus. In Pathway 3, a semi-integrated high school curriculum leading to passing of district proficiency exams, graduation requirements, or award of a certificate of attendance. Finally, in Pathway 4, a semi-integrated high school instructional program that focuses primarily on daily living skills, community-based instruction, and an award of a certificate of attendance is the focus. In all pathways, differential standards are applied as needed.

Commencement Programs

Commencement programs encourage students to experience the rite of passage of high school commencement with their peers, but continue to receive flexible and individualized transition services from the school district and in conjunction with other adult agencies and services after they meet their graduation requirements (Tashie, Malloy, & Lichtenstein, 1998). A unique aspect of commencement models is that they are entirely community-based. Just like students without disabilities, students involved in these models participate in commencement and never return to high school. Instead, these students receive their needed transition services and supports within appropriate community environments. Most commencement programs are based in an apartment, an office in a commercial district, or on postsecondary campuses such as vocational technical schools and community colleges (Morningstar et al., 1999).

MAXIMIZING THE TRANSITION POTENTIAL OF STUDENTS THROUGH SCHOOL-BASED PRACTICES

Transition for all students, especially those with disabilities, must be the goal of school systems. All professionals must be involved in preparing today's youth to live independently and be a contributing member to society. IDEA clearly specifies that schools must direct attention to outcomes and be responsible for ensuring that a planning process is in place to identify, work toward, and plan for postschool outcomes. The 1990 IDEA mandated that transition planning for students in special education begin at age 16, or younger when appropriate. According to the IDEA, transition planning must focus on students' postschool outcomes and that these outcomes be achieved through services and supports provided by a variety of agencies, not just schools. As indicated earlier, in 1994, the School-to-Work Opportunities Act (later known as School-to-Careers) was authorized. The law provided start-up funds to stimulate development of state and local partnerships between business, labor, education, and community-based organizations that would prepare and support youth to enter high-skill careers through coordination of school-based learning, work-based learning, and connecting activities between school and work (see Morningstar et al., 1999). Based on earlier indications, the 1997 reauthorization of IDEA provided the needed leverage to create secondary school reforms that will ensure successful adult outcomes for students with disabilities. Again, the unique aspects of the law that are the impetus for change in schools included (a) developing interagency linkages; (b) broadening the scope of curricula and programs to include instruction, related services, community experiences, and employment; (c) increasing performance expectations for students with disabilities in conjunction with standards-based curriculum and holding states and schools accountable for the postschool outcomes students achieve; (d) involving students, parents, and community agencies in the planning process; and (e) changing the role of many school professionals to one of service coordination. In specific terms the following practice will help to maximize the transition process of students with disabilities.

Person-Centered Planning

To facilitate the transition of students with disabilities, there must be a collaborative approach that involves a person-centered planning (PCP). PCP has emerged relatively recently as a process for facilitating the involvement of individuals with disabilities in charting their own future (Callicott, 2003). The basic tenet of PCP is to involve the individual who has a disability in a meaningful level of planning for his/her future. PCP is an effective way to increase individual, family, or community participation in the selection and design of social and educational services. This process involves a skilled facilitator addressing issues of vocation, independent or semi-independent living, recreational or leisure choices, and participation in the community (see Callicott). Working together as a team can make the transition for students with disabilities much more successful. As Callicott pointed out, PCP must be sensitive to cultural and language differences either between the dominant community and the consumer or between the consumer and primary professionals.

PCP supports both individuals and systems; and through this process, individuals, families, and communities are strengthened by the focus on respective strengths and needs (Callicott, 2003). Attention to successful communication and open-mindedness is the hallmark of the procedure. Clearly, PCP eliminates barriers and creates bridges for individuals and families who differ in some way from the normative culture. The same skilled facilitation that supports an individual who has a disability will also support an individual with a disability and cultural or language differences (see Callicott). As explained below, PCP has the strategic components of (a) group support, (b) a positive description of the student, focusing on strengths and preferences, (c) development of a vision for the future, and (d) an action plan for reaching the vision.

- *Facilitating Group Support.* Here, the student and his or her family should decide who will be involved in the person-centered planning process. The ratio of professional to nonprofessional members should be equal. Therefore, extended family members, friends, and community members must be included.
- *Creating a Positive Description.* Here, the planning is driven by the student's strengths, interests, and preferences. This positive description is developed by having the group respond to questions. Examples are: "What has he contributed to his family and community?" What are his strengths?" What does he like to do?"
- *Developing a Vision for the Future.* Here, the vision for the future should describe how the student will be fully included in the community - home, school, neighborhood, and work. While the vision for the future is positive, the person-centered planning process should not ignore obstacles and realities of service systems. It should just focus on the vision in order to make necessary changes through action planning.
- *Taking Action.* Here, the plan of action is developed based upon a dynamic and collaborative problem-solving process. This is where the planning group focuses on the barriers and obstacles to achieving the vision for the future. The action plan that is developed should include what actions will be taken, by whom, and when they will be accomplished (Morningstar et al., 1999).

Focusing on Cultural and Community Networks

Throughout the transition planning process, students should be given the opportunity and be encouraged to participate and make decisions. An IEP that includes transition planning cannot be developed unless the student has provided meaningful input. The student's preferences and interests must be included to the greatest extent possible. Successful programs that prepare students for adult living not only use school personnel but also involve members of diverse cultural communities in the preparation process (Campbell-Whatley, Algozzine, & Obiakor, 1997). Such programs focus on the culture as well as the disability. By recognizing cultural influences, teachers can better individualize services (Bakken & Aloia, 1999). Individualization should be based on disability classification and cultural context.

Postsecondary transition support programs must include a social component to promote inclusion in activities and events involving nondisabled peers. For some students, especially those with more severe disabilities, additional collaborative and consultative efforts may be needed to address difficult challenges such as low self-esteem, depression, or undeveloped social skills. One promising approach is the creation of positive "circles of support" around individuals, consisting of significant persons in their lives (e.g., friends, family, and faculty) (Cotton, Goodall, Bauer, Klein, Covert, & Nisbet, 1992). Having a support network that works positively together can prove to be a very important factor in the success of postsecondary programs. The key components of programmatic networking include (a) a focus on community outcomes when developing curriculum and instruction, (b) the importance of interagency collaboration both during planning and in formally sharing resources, (c) the necessity of an individualized method of planning for transition, and (d) the importance of family and support network involvement in planning and decision-making.

Developing Self-determination Programming

Though not consistently identified as a best practice early on, the critical role that student self-determination and student involvement play in transition planning is now considered to be a priority outcome for special education (Ward & Halloran, 1993). Halpern (1993) defined quality of life using three basic domains: (1) physical and material well-being (e.g., physical health and financial security), (2) performance of a variety of adult roles (e.g., career, leisure, personal relationships, and spiritual fulfillment), and (3) a sense of personal fulfillment (e.g., happiness, satisfaction, and a sense of general well-being). Skill development in self-advocacy and self-determination must begin early and gradually; the demands and responsibilities can be increased as the student gains competence and matures (Morningstar et al., 1999). To participate fully in their transition planning process, students should be able to advocate for their hopes, needs, and desires without undue influences from others. Students who are supported to make decisions in school, at home, on the job, and in the community are much more likely to succeed in their adult life. As Ward (1988) pointed out:

> Achieving self-determination . . . is definitely more than the sum of its parts. It requires not only that people with disabilities develop inner resources, but that society support and respond to these people. Self-determination is a lifelong interplay between the individual and society, in which the individual accepts risk-taking as a fact of life and in which the individual accepts risk-taking as a fact of life and in which society, in turn, bases an individual's worth on ability, not disability. (p 2)

Self-advocacy can best be described as the expression and fulfillment of one's needs (Phillips, 1990). If students are self-determined, they can make decisions based on their own perceptions, needs, and desires (Wehmeyer, 1998). Therefore, students must have skills and opportunities to make decisions and understand consequences of those decisions. Students who do not possess self-determination might lack the skills necessary to achieve successful adult outcomes (Martin, Marshall, & Maxon, 1993). Earlier, Wehmeyer (1992) and Ward and Halloran (1993) argued that the lack of self-determination may be one of the factors leading to poor postschool outcomes for students with disabilities. The focus on self-determination is beginning to be supported by emerging empirical data that sends a strong message of the importance associated with practices related to self-determination and student and family involvement in transition planning and service delivery (Kohler, 1996). Therefore, the four components of transition discussed below are within the framework of self-determination. First, individualized planning is a central component of self-determination because it focuses on the unique needs and aspirations of the person. However, individualized planning can facilitate self-determination only to the extent that the individual and those closest to him or her are actively involved in the process. Individualized planning that occurs in the third person (i.e., planning for the person) suggests that the person is disenfranchised from decisions about his or her long-term plans. Second, the involvement of family and support networks is at the heart of self-determination because, ultimately, the student's quality of life would depend on his or her ability to realize goals with support from those who are closest. Family involvement has emerged as one of the few consistent indicators leading to successful adult outcomes. Certainly, adolescence is a time of tremendous change for young adults and their families, particularly related to issues surrounding the emergence of adult roles and the shift from family-directed decision making to students taking the lead. Students with disabilities, however, continue to seek support and guidance from family members and friends during transition, probably more so than they do professionals. Establishing a network of support may be one of the most important features of transition planning that will ensure success long after the student leaves school. Third, a focus on community outcomes is crucial to self-determination in that it takes into account the range of contexts in which an individual will participate and allows the individual to entertain the possibilities for participation through continued learning, living arrangement and lifestyle, recreation, work and career development, and other facets of citizenship. Developing the skills to achieve successful adult outcomes is essential to implementation of transition service. How students receive the instruction should be as varied and diverse as students themselves and should be offered in a range of settings including school-based programs, community experiences, postsecondary education and training, and through natural supports and extracurricular activities. Finally, interagency collaboration provides a support network to ensure that an individual can participate and achieve the outcomes he or she chooses. The quality of interagency collaboration, however, is linked largely to how well this network supports the individual in accomplishing his or her goals.

Strategies that promote self-determination individualized planning, family and network involvement, community outcomes, and interagency collaboration must be programmatically strategized. Self-determination curricula must be infused throughout the transition process (Morningstar & Lattin, 1996). Below are specific skills taught by self-determination curricula:

- *Student Self-awareness.* Here students should be aware of their strengths, needs, interests, and preferences. They should understand their disability, learning styles, and accommodations, as well as their legal rights and responsibilities. This self-awareness must lead to increased positive self-esteem and confidence.

• *Problem-solving and Decision Making.* Here, students should define the problem, gather information and resources, identify pros and cons, make informed decisions, and communicate their preferences.

• *Goal Setting.* Here, students should learn the skills to identify their vision and long-range goals, identify all possible resources, develop an action plan to reach their goals and evaluate their outcomes. Clearly, goal setting also includes the ability to take informed risks and to take responsibility for the consequences of actions.

• *Communication Skills:* Here, these skills include body image and posture, expressing ideas and feelings, listening to what others have to say, asking questions, planning and organizing thoughts, and accepting comments and criticism.

Focusing on Successful Adult Competencies

Both school and home can provide rich opportunities for developing the skills, attitudes, and support that students need for adult survival. Students must develop these skills, at the latest, when they begin participating in their transition planning process. The 22 major competencies students need to master to become successful as adults have been identified and grouped into three major areas: daily living skills, personal-social skills, and occupational guidance and preparation (Clark & Kolstoe, 1995). See Table 2.1.

SELECTING AN APPROPRIATE TRANSITION PLAN

An appropriate plan or model should be selected and implemented to meet individual students' needs. Regardless of the chosen model, Repetto and Correa (1996) suggested that several components need to be included in this planning stage. The components include curriculum, location, futures planning, multi-agency collaboration, and a focus on family and student. See Table 2.2 for a description of these components.

Table 2.1
COMPETENCIES NEEDED TO BE SUCCESSFUL AS ADULTS

Daily Living Skills

1. Managing family finances
2. Selecting, managing, and maintaining a home
3. Caring for personal needs
4. Raising children and living as a family
5. Buying and preparing food
6. Buying and caring for clothes
7. Engaging in civic activities
8. Using recreation and leisure
9. Getting around the community (mobility)

Personal-Social Skills

10. Achieving self-awareness
11. Acquiring self-confidence
12. Achieving socially responsible behavior
13. Maintaining good interpersonal skills
14. Achieving independence
15. Achieving problem-solving skills
16. Communicating adequately with others

Occupational Guidance and Preparation

17. Knowing and exploring occupational possibilities
18. Selecting and planning occupational choices
19. Exhibiting appropriate work habits and behaviors
20. Exhibiting sufficient physical-manual skills
21. Gaining a specific occupational skill
22. Seeking, securing, and maintaining employment

Table 2.2
NEEDED TRANSITION PLAN COMPONENTS

Age	Curriculum	Location	Futures Planning	Multi-agency Collaboration	Family and Student Focus
4–15 years old	Should address academics applied to work, community, and daily living, as well as prevocational skills, socialization, independence, self-determination, and advocacy skills	Options include preschool settings, elementary schools, middle schools, and the community.	Addressed in the IEP document with transition plans that are family and student centered.	Collaboration should take place between Interagency Collaborative Councils (ICCs), school advisory councils, and agency personnel (e.g., school, work, medical, and the community).	Transition planning should be family and student centered, should support family and student input and suggestions, and provide information for support groups, and family and student advocacy.
16–21 years old	Should address academic, functional life skills, a vocational evaluation, employment skills, and independent living skills.	Options include high schools, the community, employment settings, and residential settings.	Addressed in the transition part of the IEP document and should be family and school-centered with possible postschool outcome orientation.	Collaboration should take place between ICCs, school advisory councils, agency personnel (e.g., school, work, medical, and the community) and adult service providers.	Transition planning should be family and student centered, should support family and student input and suggestions, and provide information for family and student advocacy.

FINAL THOUGHTS

In special education, transition is used to describe a systematic passage from school to adult life for students with disabilities. The IDEA provisions require that a statement of needed transition services be included in the IEP for each student beginning no later than age 16, and at a younger age if determined appropriate. In addition, IDEA provisions requested that the services be updated on an annual basis. Since the goal to provide transition programming for all students with disabilities, it behooves all professionals to prepare today's youths to be contributing members of the society through transition planning. Throughout the transition planning process, students should have the opportunity and be encouraged to participate and make decisions. Clearly, an IEP that includes transition planning cannot be developed unless the student has provided meaningful input. Both school and home can provide rich opportunities for developing the skills, attitudes, and support for self-determination. The decision of what type of plan to select and implement should be based on aspirations of the student as well as his/her parents for postschool outcomes. Each decision should be made individually to best meet the needs of all of those involved with this process.

Chapter 3

TRANSITION AND CULTURALLY AND LINGUISTICALLY DIVERSE LEARNERS

Julian, an African-American male, is 14 years old and is currently a freshman in high school. He has been diagnosed as emotionally or behaviorally disordered, with specific difficulties that include inappropriate social skills, anger problems, and disrespect for authority figures. Academically, Julian does pretty well and falls in at about the middle level when compared to his peers. He works well independently but has problems working in a group setting, taking turns, listening to others, and receiving feedback. When things do not go his way, he gets angry, verbally disruptive, shuts down completely, or does nothing. In addition, he has problems switching from one classroom to another. As a high school freshman, he needs vocational skills training to be successful after graduation based on the recommendations of his case manager, Mr. Johnson. His parents do not communicate regularly with his teacher or attend IEP meetings because they feel that teachers know what is best for their son and that teachers do not understand what it is like to be African-American. Both parents work during the school day when the IEP meetings are usually held and this gives the impression that they are nonchalant about their son's future.

How might Mr. Johnson get Julian's parents to participate in the transition planning and IEP process? What could Mr. Johnson do to learn more about African Americans and their culture? Surely, some skills are needed. This is the focus of this chapter. It is education or the world of work can be difficult for all students. Students with disabilities, however, have even more challenges and needs that must be addressed in the transition process for them to be successful. Those students who are from a nondominant group or who have cultural and linguistic differences face a double-burden. When planning transition for such students, general and special education teachers must consider the double burden syndrome when working with students and their family. Clearly, parents and students hold information vital to educators during the transition planning. Strengths, weaknesses, likes, dislikes, dreams, and hobbies are all aspects of a young person's life. All of these must be discussed and documented to design an appropriate transition plan that will benefit students in the future. To come together in a productive teaming situation, educators must learn about different cultures of their students and how to effectively communicate with different types of parents. In addition, they must understand the family structure, and develop ways to effectively communicate to ensure success for their students.

WHAT WE KNOW

The population of students in the United States is becoming increasingly more diverse, and how to meet the needs of multicultural learners with disabilities has become a major concern for teachers, school support staff, and administrators alike (Obiakor, 2004; Obiakor & Utley, 1997; Voltz, 1998). By the year 2050, the U.S. Bureau of the Census projects that culturally and linguistically diverse (CLD) groups will represent a numerical majority in the United States (Sandefur, Martin, Eggerling-Boeck, Mannon, & Meier, 2001; Sue, Bingham, Porche-Burke, & Vasquez, 1999). National statistics further reveal that an unequal number of students from ethnically, linguistically, and culturally diverse backgrounds receive special education services (Hosp & Reschly, 2004; Obiakor, Algozzine, Thurlow, Gwalla-Ogisi, Enwefa, Enwefa, & McIntosh, 2002; O'Connor, & Fernandez, 2006). Research documents that individuals who are minorities and have disabilities continue to be at risk for a number of negative outcomes including high unemployment, limited access to postsecondary education and training, low wages, limited opportunities for living independently, poor school performance, and poor participation in their respective communities (Simon, 2001). Earlier, Fillmore (1986) noted that students from diverse cultural backgrounds have lower rates of promotion at school, higher dropout rates, a greater representation in special education than other school-aged students, and lower test scores on achievement tests. As a consequence, educators must take into consideration a student's cultural differences. Put another way, in addition to a student's disability, his/her culture should also be a variable when planning transition outcomes. When cultural groups differ with respect to behavioral style, the misunderstanding of cultural behavioral style can lead to errors in estimating a student's (or group's) intellectual potential, abilities, or achievement which can directly impact decisions that will be made regarding transition plans and outcomes (Hilliard, 1992). For CLD youths with disabilities, securing desired school and post-school outcomes is particularly challenging. This is not surprising given that, in today's society, they face discrimination and oppression due to both their status as individuals with disabilities and their minority status (Simon, 2001).

Adolescents with disabilities face significant economic, educational, and community-based barriers in their transition to adulthood. In view of the multiple challenges faced by many CLD persons, it is not surprising that the initial National Longitudinal Transition Study (Blackorby & Wagner, 1996) found that, compared to non-CLD persons with disabilities, these individuals achieve significantly poorer transition outcomes, including lower average wages, lower employment rates, and lower postsecondary education participation rates. The evidence suggests that CLD students have more difficulty making postsecondary transitions than students from the dominant culture (Wilder, Jackson, & Smith, 2001). The National Longitudinal Study (see Blackorby & Wagner, 1996) revealed that African American and Hispanic American youth with disabilities have greater difficulty than European American youth with disabilities in finding employment; and when they did work, they earned significantly less than their European American counterparts. Similarly, Yelin and Trupin (1997) found that unemployed European American adults with disabilities were 40% more likely to find employment than adults with disabilities from CLD backgrounds. Interestingly, Geenan, Powers, and Lopez-Vasquez (2001) made a similar finding. Another illustration of failure to make good on commitment to individuals who are minorities with disabilities is described in Title IV of the Workforce Investment Act of 1998 (P.L. 105–220), which amended the Rehabilitation Act. Specifically, Congress found that:

Patterns of inequitable treatment of minorities have been documented in all major junctures of the vocational rehabilitation process. As compared to white Americans, a larger percentage of African-American applicants to the vocational rehabilitation system are denied acceptance. Of applicants accepted for service, a larger percentage of African-American cases are closed without being rehabilitated. Minorities are provided less training than their white counterparts. Consistently, less money is spent on minorities than on their white counterparts. (29 U.S.C. 718, Sec. 19(a)(3))

Apparently, compared to non-CLD students with disabilities, CLD students with disabilities are more likely to experience language and social barriers in the school, workforce, and community. Greene and Nefsky (1999) argued that their difficulty in processing "standard English" oral and written information and the negative effects of having grown up in poverty may contribute to their risk of school failure. Although many CLD students do transition appropriately and positively from high school, some of them have a harder time and may develop a sense of social isolation due to a "basic mismatch" between their home culture, community culture, and the educational culture commonly found in schools (Carey, Boscardin, & Fontes, 1994). These challenges are likely to be compounded for CLD students who have disabilities. As Fine and Asch (1988) concluded, they face a double burden of discrimination since they belong to two minority groups–an ethnic group as well as a disability group. A major obstacle is that most support programs for postsecondary students with disabilities focus on academic issues when the critical element in being successful is having a social support network to help maintain academic progress and promote graduation (Leake & Cholymay, 2004). Clearly, valuing diversity during transition planning is emphasized in both research and legislation (Green & Nefsky, 1999; IDEA, 1997) and needs to be implemented in schools during the transition process for CLD students with disabilities.

BEYOND KNOWLEDGE: WHAT CAN BE DONE

Teachers, support staff, and administrators are mandated to get involved with their students with disabilities in regards to the transition process. They must know if every student is getting what he/she needs to be successful when they leave the public school system. In addition, they must be aware of what students, parents, and family members are thinking regarding the transition process. Although we want students to strive to become what they want to be, we must also help them choose something possible and beneficial given their disability. Assistance is needed from parents, teachers, and guidance personnel to (a) prioritize and develop a list of individual strengths and weaknesses, (b) maximize strengths and minimize weaknesses, (c) incorporate interests and strengths into career plans, (d) develop understanding of the world of work, (e) describe and discuss differences between work and school environments, and (f) set short- and long-term goals (Michaels, Thaler, Zwerlein, Gioglio, & Apostoli, 1988). To involve diverse students with disabilities, self-determination skills can be developed and taught. The development of self-determination competencies implies that students must become actively involved in the process of the individual transition plan (ITP). While it is unclear as to how comfortable students or families are with the concept of self-determination (Miner & Bates, 1997; Trainor, 2005; Zhang & Benz, 2006), it is clear that they value the concept of self-determination, especially since they confront multidimensional problems (Bailey, Skinner, Rodriguez, Gut, & Correa, 1999). For example, teachers often maintain the misperception that CLD parents who do not attend meetings and correspond in writing do not have vested interest in their children (Voltz, 1994). In reality, passivity and compliance (via signatures on special education papers) promote feelings of powerlessness and demonstrate signs of resignation in response to frustration with the special education system rather than neglectful attitudes toward children's needs (Harry, 1992). Following are specific things that school personnel can do.

Learning About Different Cultures

It is important for teachers, support staff, and administrators to understand their students' and families cultures even if they are different from their own. Teachers, administrators, and support staff often lack the awareness, attitudes, skills, and knowledge necessary to effectively support students with disabilities. This lack may be even greater with regard to CLD students with disabilities, often due to differences in guiding cultural values (e.g., respect for authority versus personal initiative and group orientation versus individual orientation, conformity versus personal expression). In addition, some CLD students lack a high level of English proficiency as English is not their primary language in the home, although they can meet high academic standards with appropriate supports (Leake & Cholymay, 2004). Although CLD parents sometimes know more than anyone else about their own child, their insights and knowledge are devalued or ignored in the professional world by teachers, administrators, and support staff (Sanchez, 1999). As a result, many CLD families come to view the educational system as a bureaucracy controlled by educated, monocultural, monolingual individuals whom they have no power to question (Nicolau & Ramos, 1990). When oppressed and disenfranchised parents feel that their input are not important or valued they learn to not participate in the transition process as it does not matter what they say or how they feel. Additionally, teachers, administrators, and support staff make the decisions regardless of what CLD parents say or how they feel. This lack of sensitivity about diversity might cause parents to feel disengaged from schools (Adams & Welsch, 1999). Parents who are disengaged from schools tend to not participate in meetings or communicate ineffectively with others on school-related issues. By not being sensitive to parents' feelings, attitudes, perceptions, knowledge, and culture, teachers, administrators, and school staff create a barrier to effective support and communication and parent-school partnerships. To a large extent, relationships are built when educational professionals gain cultural and linguistic competency, encourage or support parents, reduce conflict belief systems, eliminate racial discrimination, and value immigrant parents' experiences (Adames, 2000; Basterra, 1998; Jones & Velez, 1997).

School personnel working with CLD parents of students with disabilities must be aware of the cultural differences that might exist between them and these families. To change their values and beliefs, school personnel need to be aware that everyone does not come from the same culture, nor do they all behave or act the same way in the home or community. A person's own culture can be very influential in how a person reacts, communicates, and socializes with others. Awareness of multicultural issues begins with a personal examination of one's own beliefs, values, and possible biases (Sue & Sue, 1999). Lynch and Hanson (1992) recommended that special educators and other professionals listen more, observe family communication patterns, slow down, be aware of nonverbal behaviors or gestures, and consult cultural guides or mediators when interacting with members of these various CLD groups. It is not uncommon to see educational professionals as "outsiders," especially when they are patronizing or paternalistic. Parents sometimes feel that because their children were singled out for special services, these professionals must have a problem with them. Involving parents and the community in the planning and implementation of programs designed to assist students can facilitate effective intervention efforts and reduce the likelihood of mutual distrust (Wilder et al., 2001). In addition, team members must have an open mind to all aspirations or desires of the individual, family, and community when plans are being developed. Regardless of how trivial or unlikely those desires may appear to professionals it is important to understand the needs of those involved (De Carvalho, 2001). In the same dimension, it is critical to provide CLD learners with opportunities to practice skills required of them to be successful in the community before they actually become independent community members.

Considering Family and Cultural Values

It is very apparent that to make a successful transition plan for a CLD student with a disability general and special educators must include the student as well as his/her family. To do this effectively, they must consider the family and cultural values to the best of their abilities. Who knows more about the child than the parents and family? Combes and Durodoye (2007) noted that parental involvement is an important factor in promoting the successful programming for youth with disabilities into adulthood. Parental participation is particularly important for CLD youth since a strong partnership between parents and the school can promote cultural understanding and responsiveness in transition planning. Bakken and Aloia (1999) agreed that when educators engage in a firm partnership with parents, they can more effectively meet the needs of their CLD students. Parents need to be a part of the transition process as well as teachers and the community. All participants need to collaborate to develop an effective transition plan for the student. This means that everyone must acknowledge and accept the thoughts, ideas, and feelings of others when developing the transition plan for the diverse child with disabilities. Clearly, collaboration must be emphasized in promoting the successful transition of youth with disabilities into adulthood. Earlier,

Schalock, Wolzen, Ross, Elliott, Werbel, and Peterson (1986), in studying youth with learning or developmental disabilities, found that students whose parents were actively involved in transition programming were more successful on employment outcome measures than students whose parents had little involvement. Obviously, parents hold a wealth of knowledge about their child and are an important piece of developing an effective transition plan. Youth who had high family involvement worked more hours and received higher wages than students who had low family involvement (Geenan et al., 2001). Everson and Moon (1987) maintained that parents and family members are the only people to have continuous and stable contact with the student throughout the entire process. Clearly, parents and family members should be equal partners with the school and other agencies involved in the planning process (Navarrete & White, 1994). Yet, the participation of CLD parents in special education programs is even less involved and less informed than that of mainstream parents (Hanley-Maxwell, Pogoloff, & Whitney-Thomas, 1998; Harry, 1992).

General and special educators need to bridge the gap that has been created between schools and parents/families. Involving interested family and friends in school-to-work transitions improves employment outcomes for students with disabilities (Hasazi, Gordon, & Roe, 1985). In fact, family and community assistance is considered a best practice in effective transition programs (Kilburn & Critchlow, 1998; Kohler, 1993); these individuals can help students to find jobs, teach them what they need to do to be successful at the job, and support them when times are tough (Wilder et al., 2001). All of these individuals must collaborate and consult to facilitate the transition process because most students find employment through parental or community-based networks (see Hasazi et al., 1985). Voltz (1998) confirmed that poor families expend a greater proportion of energy, time, and resources just trying to meet their basic needs. In addition, to the built-in stress factors of just being a parent, there are the realities of having a child with a disability. Finally, being different in a society that does not always view differences as a positive attribute can be very stressful. These inhibitors exhaust the resources of parents from CLD backgrounds. As Voltz summarized ". . . these parents may not always be physically, emotionally, or cognitively available to participate as vigorously in the education of their children as educators—and, perhaps they themselves—would desire" (Voltz, p. 65). The issue of parental involvement must be faced directly. If successful transition is dependent upon parents actively working with schools and if parents do not become involved due to cultural differences, schools are faced with a major dilemma. Earlier, Halpern (1992) captured this conundrum very concisely when he wrote:

> If our needed educational reform can only be accomplished with the assistance of parents, and if some parents want to abdicate this responsibility, and if policymakers are afraid or unwilling to confront the issue, many of the problems that currently bedevil the schools will remain unresolved. Students with disabilities, of course, will be caught up in the vortex of these unresolved problems, which must inevitably have an impact on opportunities that are available within special education and transition programs whether or not parents of students with disabilities are actively involved in these programs. (pp. 210–211)

It is well known that parental involvement in the education of children improves the well-being of families, enhances parenting skills, and improves educational results for children. It is no surprise that IDEA requires parental participation in identification and assessment processes. CLD parents must be provided with information to ensure that they understand the special education placement proceedings and decisions. While all parents of children with disabilities may face some barriers to parental involvement, some inner-city parents of children with disabilities may face obstacles due to limited English proficiency, cultural factors, or the effects of poverty. For example, many parents of English language learners do not speak English fluently and may not understand technical terms used during special educational assessments and individualized education plan (IEP) meetings. In the end, they feel inadequate when speaking to special education or school personnel, partly due to their inability to speak English (Santos & Santos, 1984).

MAKING THE TRANSITIONAL PROCESS WORK
WITH CLD PARENTS

To better involve the student and family in the transition process, school professionals must first acknowledge some barriers to collaboration that get in the way of effective communication and collaboration. Perceived barriers to collaboration include (a) scheduling meetings at times inconvenient for parents (Linan-Thompson & Jean, 1997); (b) conveying information about services and parents' rights through written materials in English higher than a fifth-grade reading level to families with limited literacy skills (Leung, 1996) or to non-English speaking immigrants who may not be literate even in their native language (Weiss & Coyne, 1997); and (c) little effort on the part of professionals to seek families' input when making decisions about their child's education (Harry, Allen, & McLaughlin, 1995). In addition, families' economic and cultural circumstances can contribute to low parental involvement; increased communication and language barriers (Heller, Markwardt, Rowitz, & Farber, 1994; Leung, 1996); lack of transportation and/or child care (Kalyanpur & Rao, 1991); cultural misinterpretation in help-seeking behavior (Danseco, 1997); historically poor relationships with schools (Thorp, 1997); negative beliefs about disability (Danseco, 1997); and poor perceptions of professionals as experts (Harry et al., 1995). Culturally sensitive special education services can enhance the likelihood of successful postsecondary transitions since cultures influence postsecondary outcomes (Bakken & Aloia, 1999). By recognizing cultural influences, teachers can better individualize services. This individualization should be based on disability classification and cultural context. Knowing the cultural context in which a student lives and works helps the teacher or service provider to determine social skills and vocabulary that must be mastered during transition.

During IEP/ITP meetings, parents and students may vary in their levels of comfort in accepting a central planning role, especially if they view educators as having higher status. This will likely influence the scope of their participation, as well as their expectations of one another. Parents may be uncomfortable allowing their child to play a leadership role in a meeting of adults and professionals (Miner & Bates, 1997), although Wehmeyer (1998) highlights that there are benefits of involving students with disabilities in the planning that include (a) an enhanced motivation to learn, (b) improved educational outcomes, and (c) opportunities to learn and practice self-advocacy skills. Earlier, Turnbull and Winton (1984) explained that, to be influential advocates, parents need extensive familiarity with legal mandates and available services, technical knowledge about assertive confrontation, and communication skills. Parents with little education and limited English proficiency may find participation in school programs particularly difficult. As a result, some parents (i.e., Latino parents) may assume a passive role in the educational decision making process (Turnbull & Turnbull, 2000). Morningstar, Turnbull, and Turnbull (1996) conducted a qualitative study using focus groups to explore student perspectives on family involvement in the transition from school to adult life and found that families help students develop a future vision related to career and lifestyle options, and supports needed to live on their own. Students also mentioned that planning should begin earlier in their schooling and that they saw no link between the IEP and their futures out of school.

It is important for teachers and other professionals to learn about and accept the culture of the child and family. "As the experimental gap between teachers and their successes increases, so does teachers' fear of crossing what they perceive as barriers to communication with poor families, and, in particular, families from racial groups other than their own" (Harry, Torguson, Katkavich, & Guerrero, 1993, p. 48). This needs to be done if general and special educators want the child to experience success. Another way to involve the family might be the involvement of a mentor. According to Campbell-Whatley, Obiakor, and Algozzine (1997), a mentor can encourage the participation of parents by building a connection with the student's family. Mentorship programs where volunteers are paired with students can be effective. Mentors can stimulate the students' thinking and help them progress towards their goals while improving self-esteem. As Campbell-Whatley et al. pointed out, mentoring programs are effective when proactive efforts are made to:

- Identify and select program staff to direct students.
- Refine program goals and objectives to improve students' behaviors.
- Define a target population to know students.
- Develop activities and procedures to direct students' contacts.
- Orientate mentors and students to understand students' roles.
- Monitor mentoring progress to address students' problems.
- Manage the matching process to ensure students' communication.
- Evaluate program effectiveness to monitor students' progress.

FINAL THOUGHTS

With the increase of diverse students in our schools fast approaching a numerical majority, the number of students with disabilities from this population will also increase. It has become clear that CLD individuals with disabilities continue to be at risk for high unemployment, limited access to postsecondary education and training, low wages, limited opportunities for living independently, and poor school performance. Since transition services for these individuals are very important and much needed, teachers, support staff, and administrators need to get involved in the transition process. To do this, they must understand their students' and families' cultures to maximize their potential to survive in a competitive society like ours. In addition, they must be aware of the cultural differences that might exist between them and their families. We know that families hold a wealth of knowledge about their child. It is critical that general and special educators empower them and their communities. We must listen to the voices of CLD youth with disabilities and increase their ability to enter into dialogue and engage in their world. Finally, we must ensure that local policies and procedures to support the development of leadership and self-determination skills in students are in place and implemented in the community.

Chapter 4

SELECTING APPROPRIATE ASSISTIVE TECHNOLOGY FOR STUDENT TRANSITION

John is 17 years old and is a junior in high school. He has an educational diagnosis of a learning disability, with difficulties in reading and organizational skills. He often forgets to complete his assignments and has trouble remembering to bring materials needed for class, especially for special projects or assignments. John reads at the fourth grade level, but has good auditory comprehension skills. He has strong math and problem-solving skills as well. John's parents are very supportive and communicate regularly with his teachers and case manager; however, John has learned to advocate effectively for himself as well. After high school, John plans to attend a junior college for two years and then transfer to a university. He wants to pursue a bachelor's degree in Recreational Program Management in order to work as a coordinator of recreational programs within a park district or similar type of agency. John has experience working as a counselor at a children's summer sports camp and currently works at an after-school program run by the local park district.

Based on the above case, what types of assistive technology could help students like John to be successful in high school, postsecondary education, and his future career? This chapter responds to this critical question. It is common knowledge that planning the transition from high school to postsecondary education or the world of work can be difficult for all students. Students with disabilities, however, have even more challenges and needs that must be addressed in the transition process in order for those students to be successful. Involving assistive technology in the transition planning, and the transition process itself, can be beneficial for many students with disabilities (Kim-Rupnow & Burgstahler, 2004; Morgan, Gerity, & Ellerd, 2000; Mull & Sitlington, 2003; Nochajski, Oddo, & Beaver, 1999). Since both transition planning and assistive technology evaluation are mandated for students with disabilities, it is logical for IEP teams to address how assistive technology could help students prepare for and make successful transitions.

ASSISTIVE TECHNOLOGY: DEFINITIONS AND CONCEPTUALIZATIONS

Assistive technology (AT) is defined in the IDEA Amendments of 1997 as "any item, piece of equipment, or product system, whether acquired commercially off the shelf, modified, or customized, that is used to increase, maintain, or improve the functional capabilities of a child with a disability" [P.L. 105–17, Section 602 (1)]. A more functional definition of AT is: *any tool that allows a person to perform a task that he/she would otherwise be unable to perform or perform as effectively.* AT can enable people with disabilities to accomplish daily living tasks, assist them in communication, educational, vocational, or recreational activities and, as a result, help them achieve greater independence and a better quality of life. An assistive technology service, as stated in IDEA 1997, is "any service that directly assists a child with a disability in the selection, acquisition, or use of an assistive technology device. Such term includes:

(A) the evaluation of the needs of such child, including a functional evaluation of the child in the child's customary environment;
(B) purchasing, leasing, or otherwise providing for the acquisition of assistive technology devices by such child;
(C) selecting, designing, fitting, customizing, adapting, applying, maintaining, repairing, or replacing of assistive technology devices;
(D) coordinating and using other therapies, interventions, or services with assistive technology devices, such as those associated with existing education and rehabilitation plans and programs;
(E) training or technical assistance for such child, or, where appropriate, the family of such child; and

(F) training or technical assistance for professionals (including individuals providing education and rehabilitation services), employers, or other individuals who provide services to, employ, or are otherwise substantially involved in the major life functions of such child. [P.L. 105–17, Section 602 (2)]

These aspects of AT services must go hand-in-hand with the chosen AT, in order for the utilization of that AT device to be effective. Since IDEA 1997 mandated that IEP teams evaluate the assistive technology needs of all students with disabilities and address any identified needs in the IEP [P. L. 105–17, Section 1414 (d)(3)(B)(v)], it is imperative that those IEP teams address not only the specific AT that a student needs, but also any AT services that are necessary to incorporate the AT devices into the child's life both at home and at school.

When people picture assistive technology devices, they often envision computers or various types of complicated electronic devices. It is important to realize, however, that assistive technology devices actually exist on a continuum that ranges from "no-tech" to "high-tech." When selecting AT devices for a student, it is important to consider all types of technology that could benefit that student, beginning with the "no-tech" or "low-tech" devices and working up through the continuum until the appropriate type(s) of AT for the student is determined.

No-Tech Devices

No-tech options are those that involve the use or adaptation of policies, procedures, services, and existing conditions in the environment and do *not* involve the use of additional devices or equipment. Some examples of "no-tech" options could include utilizing services such as physical therapy and occupational therapy. Examples of adaptations of policies and procedures are: (a) giving a student shortened assignments; (b) allowing for additional time for the student to move from class to class, and (c) extending the amount of time given for an assignment. Since "no-tech" options usually do not involve the need for training or additional funding, they can be implemented more easily and quickly in the educational setting.

Low-Tech Devices

Low-tech items are less sophisticated, less expensive, and are usually more readily available for purchase and use. These devices typically require little structured training in order to use the device correctly and effectively. Examples of low-tech devices include adapted spoon handles, nontipping drinking cups, pencil grips, and Velcro fasteners.

High-Tech Devices

High-tech devices incorporate sophisticated devices that typically include electronics or computers. These devices usually require training for proper use and can be more expensive and complex. Examples of high-tech devices are voice recognition software, speech synthesizers, and adaptations to computers for accessibility.

PROVIDING THE TECHNOLOGY CONTINUUM TO STUDENTS WITH DISABILITIES

In making decisions about the type of technology tools a particular person might require, a good approach is to start with the no-tech solutions and then work up the continuum, as needed. When making technology decisions, teams often start at the "high-tech" end of the technology continuum when, in fact, it is better to start at a lower point. For example, when making decisions about a person whose handwriting is difficult to read, recommendations could be made that a laptop computer that can be taken to various environments in which written products are required should be purchased. Realistically, an electronic keyboard with memory that can be later downloaded onto a computer may be more appropriate for the student. This could mean a large difference in cost, and would be just as effective for the student (NATRI, 2004). The following example shows the steps that can be taken to examine a student's AT needs and match those needs with the appropriate and least intrusive technology from the continuum.

Paul had difficulty with written work due to difficulty with holding and maneuvering a writing utensil. The IEP team decided to address this problem by adding a pencil grip to the student's pencil (low-tech) to help with correct finger positioning. This did not seem to alleviate the problem, due to the amount of writing that was necessary in the student's classes. Therefore, the team chose to train the student to use a personal word processor or electronic keyboard (medium-tech) so the student could type instead of writing words by hand. This option also seemed ineffective in alleviating the writing problem for the student, so the team selected a speech-to-text software program (high-tech) that the student could use on a laptop computer to speak instead of writing or typing. This way, the student could be more independent with writing notes and doing written assignments for his classes.

It is important that IEP teams think of the entire continuum of AT devices that are available and effective for their students. If teams select only high-tech options, the AT may be inappropriate or ineffective for the student, the task, or the setting, and, as a result, the costly device could sit unused. In addition, if the student is not included in the selection process or if there is no training given to the student, family, and professionals working with the AT device, the AT will be less likely to be effective for the student, or even used at all (Burgstahler, 2003; Reimer-Reiss & Wacker, 2000; Wielandt & Scherer, 2004).

Services by School District

IDEA (1997) includes a listing of the services that a school district may need to provide, in order to ensure that the selected AT is appropriate and beneficial to students within their school setting. These services could include any or all of the following possibilities (see Parents Let's Unite for Kids, 2004):

- Evaluation of technology needs of the individual, including a functional evaluation within the individual's typical environment.
- Purchasing, leasing, or otherwise providing for the acquisition of AT devices for individuals with an IEP.
- Selecting, designing, adjusting, adapting, maintaining, repairing, or replacing of AT devices.
- Coordinating and using other therapies, interventions, or services with the AT devices, according to the IEP.

- Training or technical assistance with AT for the individual and/or the family of the individual with disabilities.
- Training or technical assistance for professionals, employers, or other individuals who provide services to or employ individuals with disabilities.

These services are important when it comes to the process of evaluating a student for AT needs, selecting appropriate AT for the student, training the student, his/her family, and education professionals working with that student, and evaluating how well the AT is working and other needs of the student. It is helpful to utilize an AT selection framework during this process, in order to ensure that all needs are addressed, all viewpoints and expertise are shared, and that all options are considered.

SETT Framework. A simple and straightforward framework that can be used for evaluating students' AT needs and selecting AT devices is the SETT Framework (Zabala, 1996). The framework has four basic parts–**S**tudent, **E**nvironment, **T**asks, and **T**ools–and can be used as an organizational tool for IEP teams and other collaborative groups working with students with special needs. The variety of knowledge, expertise, and experiences that members of these teams bring to the table, along with the organization of the SETT Framework, will enhance the quality of the AT evaluation and selection process. See Table 4.1 for a description of the four main areas included in the SETT Framework.

Table 4.1
SETT Framework–Category Descriptions

STUDENT	• Characteristics • Strengths • Weaknesses • Present levels of performance
ENVIRONMENT	• Where student is expected to function • What is used in that environment • Expectations for students • Supports already available to students and staff
TASKS	• Prerequisite skills needed • Required activities for students • Related tasks (i.e., communication)
TOOLS	• Necessary devices to meet students' needs(low to high-tech) • Necessary services to meet students' needs or to use AT devices effectively

The four main parts of the SETT Framework correspond to essential areas that should be addressed in an AT evaluation (see Table 4.1). When examining each area, some basic questions can help to guide IEP teams as they evaluate a student's needs for AT. See Table 4.2 for a list of these guiding questions and additional steps that teams can use during their AT evaluations to gain a clearer picture of each student's needs within their current environments. It is important to remember, however, that these questions are a guide for discussions, and other questions may arise that need to be addressed in order to make an informed decision about a particular student's needs for AT devices and services. (More information about the SETT Framework is available at http://www.joyzabala.com.)

Since AT evaluation is mandated to be part of the students' IEP programming, it is likely that many students will have already been evaluated regarding their AT needs in the classroom. Some of the needs already identified and addressed will continue to be needs within the context of transition; however, transition planning would also be the time to begin evaluating the students' needs for AT in the workplace, postsecondary education, at home, and to function within the community more independently. The earlier in the transition planning process that student needs are identified and appropriate AT is selected to meet those needs the better off the student will be. This way students can try out the AT device to select the most appropriate one for their needs, be trained to use the selected AT devices effectively, and, as a result, be better prepared when they graduate from high school (Stodden, Conway, & Chang, 2003). Table 4.3 contains valuable resources to help teams through this evaluation process, including steps to follow and forms to document each part of the evaluation, selection, and re-evaluation processes.

PROCESS OF CHOOSING THE MOST APPROPRIATE TECHNOLOGY

Remember John, the student learned about at the beginning of this chapter! How might his IEP team go about determining his needs? How might those needs be best addressed using assistive technology? Let's walk through a brief version of the SETT Framework using John

Table 4.2
SETT Framework–Guiding Questions

The Student
- What is the functional area(s) of concern? (What does the student need to be able to do that is difficult or impossible to do independently at this time?)
- What are the student's special needs related to the area(s) of concern?
- What are the student's current capabilities related to the area(s) of concern?

The Environments
- What is the physical arrangement of the environment(s) that the child must function within? The instructional arrangements?
- What types of support are available within this environment(s) to the student and to the staff?
- What materials and/or equipment are commonly used within the environment(s)?
- What types of access issues (technological, physical, instructional) exist for the student in the environment(s)?
- What are the attitudes and expectations of the staff, family, and others within the environment(s) for the student?

The Tasks
- What SPECIFIC tasks occur in the student's natural environments that enable progress toward mastery of IEP goals and objectives?
- What SPECIFIC tasks are required for a student's active involvement in the identified environments within the following areas: communication, instruction, participation, productivity, and environmental control?

The Tools
**Analyze the information gathered on the student, environment, and tasks to address the following questions and steps.
- Is it expected that the student will not be able to make reasonable progress toward his/her educational goals without AT devices and services?
- If yes, describe what a useful and effective system of AT devices and services for this student would look like.
- Brainstorm possible tools that could be included in this system to address the student's needs.
- Select the most appropriate and promising tools for trials in the student's natural environments.
- Plan out the specifics of the trial for the AT devices and services (i.e., when and how the tools will be used, necessary cues for the student, follow-up, etc.).
- Collect data on the effectiveness of the device and make any necessary modifications.
- Continue to evaluate the student's needs and effectiveness of the AT devices and services being used to determine any changes that need to be made.

Adapted from Zabala, J. (2002, March). A brief introduction to the SETT Framework. Retrieved October 11, 2004 from http://www.joyzabala.com.

Table 4.3
Helpful Resources and Tools for Evaluating and Selecting AT Devices and Services

Name of Organization or Resource	Web Address	Description of Resources
Wisconsin Assistive Technology Initiative	http://wati.org/pdf/attransitionpacket.pdf	This packet contains information, a timeline for transition planning, and forms that can be used when evaluating and planning for AT and transition.
SETT Forms, Consideration Forms, and Implementation & Evaluation Planning Guide	http://sweb.uky.edu/~jszaba0/JoysHandouts.html	These forms and planning guide can help with evaluating and planning for the use of AT devices. They can also assist with the on-going evaluation of AT device effectiveness and student needs.
Learning Disabilities On-Line	http://www.ldonline.org/ld_indepth/technology/evaluation.pdf	This form and planning guide can help teams look at AT needs in various curricular areas, which could carry over into postsecondary education settings.

as an example in order to better understand how to use the SETT Framework to assist in the evaluation and selection process. This example is not the only "right answer" for John, as many variables need to be evaluated, and devices would need to be tried out, in order to determine his "best fit."

Step 1–Use the Framework to Evaluate John's Needs

Using the guiding questions listed in Table 4.2, the team would look at John's specific needs, as well as the demands within his environment that could be related to or affected by his needs. The team would then look at the tasks that John is required to complete, to participate fully in the classroom. This information would then be summarized on the form, The SETT Framework–Part I, and the barriers to John's progress that need to be addressed through the use of AT would also be identified on that form.

In John's case, the team noted his areas of strength and concern under the "Student" heading on the form, such as his auditory comprehension strength and his lower reading comprehension skills. Team members also noted John's transition goals under the "Student" heading to keep those goals in focus as they completed the remainder of the form. The team then looked at the environment that John currently functions in at school, as well as what could be expected posthigh school environment, and listed these aspects under the "Environments" heading on the form. Finally, the team looked at what activities are required of ALL students in the classes John is taking currently, and summarized those under the "Tasks" heading. In addition, the team listed tasks that could be expected of him in college courses, as well as in the workplace in that section. An annotated SETT Framework–Part I form, as well as an example of what this form could look like for John is given below.

Step 2–Brainstorm Possible Devices That Could Meet John's Needs

Next, the team would identify a list of possible AT devices and services that could be used to address John's needs as determined in Part I. The SETT Framework–Part II-A form would then be used to identify important functions or elements within each area of need, organize the list of possible AT devices and services, and mark which specific function(s) could be addressed by each AT device or service listed. A separate form would be used to further evaluate each identified area of need.

The team evaluating John's AT needs decided that there were five main areas, or functions, that needed to be addressed: reading fluency, reading comprehension of textbook material, reading on-screen information, reading other materials (i.e., newspapers and magazines), and reading for tests. After determining those functions, they discussed many different types of AT, from low to high-tech devices, and came

ANNOTATED SETT FRAMEWORK - PART I

Collaboratively Gathering and Analyzing Information from a Variety of Sources

Student: _____ Date: _____ Perspective: _____

EXAMINING CURRENT CONDITIONS TO ESTABLISH EDUCATIONAL NEED		
STUDENT	**ENVIRONMENTS**	**TASKS**
INFORMATION RELATED SPECIFICALLY TO THE STUDENT. INCLUDING SPECIFIC AREAS OF CONCERN, SPECIAL NEEDS, CURRENT ACHIEVEMENT, INTERESTS, GOALS, ETC. • Build shared knowledge about the student that can be used to identify need for tools, guide decisions about tools, and assist in planning implementation and evaluation of effectiveness. • Determine what still needs to be known and how it can be found out. • Add additional information as it becomes available through evaluation, implementation, or discussion	INFORMATION RELATED TO ANYONE WHO IS AROUND THE STUDENT OR ANYTHING THAT IS PROVIDED TO THE STUDENT. • Build shared knowledge about the environments in which the student is, or can be, expected to learn and grow. This information can be used to identify need for environmental supports and training, and assist in planning implementation and evaluation of effectiveness. • Determine what still needs to be known and how it can be found out. • Add additional information as it becomes available through evaluation, implementation or discussion	INFORMATION SPECIFICALLY RELATED TO THE DETAILS OF THE TASKS THAT ARE CURRENTLY REQUIRED OF THE STUDENT OR WILL BE REQUIRED IN THE NEAR FUTURE. • Build shared knowledge about the tasks that the student needs to do or learn to do that are currently difficult or impossible for the student to do at the expected level of independence. • This information can be used to identifying the type of tools needed, but will also play a critical role in planning implementation and evaluation of effectiveness. • Determine what still needs to be known and how it can be found out. • Add additional information as it becomes available through evaluation, implementation, discussion.

• CIRCLE FUNCTIONAL AREA(S) OF CONCERN
• UNDERLINE BARRIERS TO STUDENT PROGRESS
• STAR SUPPORTS FOR STUDENT PROGRESS

THE SETT FRAMEWORK - PART I
Collaboratively Gathering and Analyzing Information from a Variety of Sources

Student: ___John___ Date: _____ Perspective: _____

DESCRIBE CURRENT CONDITIONS TO ESTABLISH EDUCATIONAL NEED		
STUDENT	**ENVIRONMENTS**	**TASKS**

-Eligible for sp ed due to learning disability
-Difficulty remembering assignments and needed materials for his classes
-Reading decoding & comprehension skills are an area of concern:
  -Reads at a 5th grade level
  -Recall is low when he reads aloud or to himself
-Much better comprehension (92% recall) when information is presented orally (auditory comp.)
-Math skills and problem-solving skills are at grade level
**Displays good self-advocacy skills
**Has work experience at a park district sports camp and currently works at the park district with the after school program
TRANSITION GOALS:
-Complete Associate's degree at a junior college & then transfer to a university
-Study Recreational Program Management to become a coordinator of recreational programs at a park district or similar agency
	CURRENT:
	-General education classrooms with support from a special education teacher in English
	-Participates in the general education curriculum with some adaptations/ modifications
	-Participates in a Vocational Ed./Work Program (works at the park district)
	-John meets with his case manager once a week to check on his grades, progress, and any needs
	**Adaptations include: books on tape, tests read, extra time for tests and shorter reading assignments
	
	POST HIGH SCHOOL:
	-Will participate in junior college and univ. courses
	**Supports are available for students with disabilities–must be accessed by student
	-Student-led support–teachers will not necessarily check in with him
	-Plans to work in a park district or similar agency after college
		CURRENT:
		-Reading assignments (textbooks, novels, worksheets)
		-Taking notes from overheads and chalkboards
		-Group projects in various classes
		-Writing assignments (research papers, short essays, worksheets, journals)
		-Algebra assignments (computation & word problems)
		-Tests & quizzes (reading component)
		-Work program logs and reflections; additional vocational ed assignments (reading & worksheets)
		
		POST-HIGH SCHOOL:
		-Reading assignments (textbooks, novels, worksheets, articles, internet resources)
		-Writing assignments (research papers, journals, other written work)
		-Math assignments (based on course taken)
		-Tests & quizzes (various types of questions)
		-Reading and writing tasks associated with coordinating rec programs

• UNDERLINE BARRIERS TO STUDENT PROGRESS
• STAR SUPPORTS FOR STUDENT PROGRESS

THE SETT FRAMEWORK - PART II

Develop Descriptors of an Assistive Technology Tool System that Addresses Needs and Identify Possible Tools

STUDENT: _____John_____ AREA OF ESTABLISHED NEED (See SETT: Part I): _____Reading Skills_____

STEP 1: Based on SETT data, enter descriptors or functions needed by the student across the shaded top row - 1 descriptor per column
STEP 2: Enter promising tools in the shaded left column - 1 tool per row
STEP 3: For each tool, note matches with descriptors and functions to help guide discussion of devices and services
USE ADDITIONAL SHEETS IF NECESSARY

Descriptors → Tools ↓	Reading Fluency	Reading comprehension to textbook material	Reading on-screen information (Internet etc)	Reading other materials (newspapers, magazines, etc)	Reading for tests				
Books on Tape		X							
Reading Pen	X	X		X	X				
Screen Reader			X						
Text to Speech software	X	X	X	X	X				
Portable word scanner	X	X		X	X				

© Joy Zabala (Revised 2004) PERMISSION TO USE GRANTED IF CREDITS ARE MAINTAINED
SETT Forms and additional resources are available for download at http://www.joyzabala.com. Please provide feedback on effectiveness and suggestions for modifications/revisions by email to joy@joyzabala.com

THE SETT FRAMEWORK - PART II - B

Establishing Availability and Training Needs for Promising Tools

SHORT LIST OF TOOLS	TOOL AVAILABILITY			SERVICES (training, planning, coordination, etc) REQUIRED FOR EFFECTIVE USE		
JUSTIFY CHOICES WITH SETT DATA AND DESCRIPTOR MATCH	S	P	A	STUDENT	STAFF	FAMILY
Books on Tape (for textbooks) This will help John with the large amount of textbook reading that is required and will continue to be required in his postsecondary education. Since his auditory comprehension is good, this would be an effective support.		X		-Access to tape player and headphones -Training on the process for ordering the textbooks, so student can order after H.S.	-Provide for a space and appropriate time within each class period for the student to use the tapes -Provide tape player and headphones for student	-Training on ordering tapes, in order to assist student after H.S.
Reading Pen This device is easy to carry and can be used with any type of print, including tests, to support John's reading. The device reads the words aloud which will help him with comprehension. This device can also be used in his postsecondary education and even into his career to support him with his reading requirements			X	-Training on the use and maintenance of the device -Time for practice and ongoing evaluation of the effectiveness of the device	-Training on the use and maintenance of the device -Plan for the use of device in the classroom without disruption to the class or the student -Evaluation of the effectiveness of the device	-Training on the use and maintenance of the device -Work with family on funding sources in order to acquire the device themselves for John's use after H.S.
Text to Speech software This device is more complex, but can be used for any type of print material, including on-screen reading material. John can use this software to aid in his comprehension of material in H.S., post secondary education, and in his career, due to the auditory component and the text highlighting features.			X	-Access to a computer for use of software -Training & practice for proper use of the software -Copies of software available for home and school	-Training for all John's teachers on the use of the software program -Planning for the use of the program within each of John's classrooms -Make computer(s) available that have the program	-Training for proper use and maintenance of the software -Work with family on funding sources in order to acquire the program themselves for John's use after H.S.

KEY: S = Systemically available tools - Currently available to ALL students served by this system
    P = Programmatically available through special education services or other services for which identified student is qualified
    A = Additional tools that need to be acquired for this student.

© Joy Zabala (Revised 2004) PERMISSION TO USE GRANTED IF CREDITS ARE MAINTAINED
SETT Forms and additional resources are available for download at http://www.joyzabala.com. Please provide feedback on effectiveness and suggestions for modifications/revisions by email to joy@joyzabala.com

up with five that seemed possible for John. Then, they looked at which functions each of these devices could realistically address, based on each device's capabilities. See the following form for an example of this process, using reading as the area of need.

Step 3-Select the Most Appropriate Devices/System for John

After the team determines which AT devices from their list would be most beneficial and appropriate for John, the SETT Framework-Part II-B form would be used to map out the availability of each device, as well as services required for the student, staff, and family to utilize each tool effectively. These services could include training needs, changes to the schedule or classroom procedures that would be necessary for use of the device, and any other maintenance and on-going evaluation needs.

For John, the team decided that a combination of three AT devices would best help him to complete all of the tasks with which he has difficulty: books on tape (audio text), a reading pen, and text to speech software. The benefits of these devices, as well as how they would assist John are described on the form as well. The team then looked at the availability of each, and determined that two of the three would have to be acquired for John specifically. They also discussed what services would be needed for the student, the staff, and the family to use the devices correctly and effectively, and put those needs in writing on the form as well. See the following form below for this example. [*Note: Devices listed are general categories and not specific device names. There are several choices of specific devices within these general categories.*]

USEFUL WEB RESOURCES FOR ASSISTIVE TECHNOLOGY

The area of AT is expanding daily and it can be difficult to keep up with all the information regarding this area. As this part of our field expands, it becomes more and more difficult to keep abreast with everything that is available or at your disposal. The whole process of coming up with AT alternatives and possibilities can be a bit over-whelming for any IEP team no matter what their experience. There is, however, a constant supply of AT products, information, training, and research available right at your fingertips.

Assistive Technology Products

There are many AT products available that could possibly benefit students with disabilities to transition from high school to post-secondary education or the world of work. New products are being introduced daily and it can be difficult to keep up with all of the new and old products available. Table 4.4 contains some useful web resources to help teachers, parents, and other professionals learn more about AT products.

Table 4.4
Assistive Technology Products

ABLEDATA www.abledata.com
The ABLEDATA database has information on many assistive technology products for a variety of different needs. The database includes detailed descriptions of each product including price and company information, as well as information on prototypes, customized, and one-of-a-kind products. They do not produce or sell any of the products listed on the database themselves, but provide information on how to contact manufacturers or distributors of the products. The site also contains a Consumer Forum with reviews of products from people who have used them and a Reading Room with information on assistive technology.

Ability Hub www.abilityhub.com
The Ability Hub website has AT devices, adaptive equipment, and alternative methods for people with disabilities that have difficulty operating a computer. The devices are categorized by disability area and specific uses. The site also includes a "Link of Interest," an "E-column," and answers to frequently asked questions about AT and specific AT devices.

Assis-TECH http://www.assis-tech.com
The Assis-TECH website contains assistive technology devices and ADA compliant adjustable furniture that can be purchased on-line or over the phone. They offer specialty computer hardware, software, and assistive technology input and output devices designed for people who are physically disabled, hearing impaired, visually impaired, and/or learning disabled. The site also includes an on-line newsletter with current information on laws and new devices.

Enablemart www.enablemart.com
The EnableMart website contains lists of available AT devices in the areas of communication, hearing, mobility, keyboards/mice, vision, switches, and workstations. EnableMart carries over 1500 assistive technology and assistive living devices from over 150 manufacturers, and these products are available for demonstration or purchase through their website, catalog, sales office, or retail/demo center. The site also includes information on "hot" AT devices, links of interest, and an upcoming AT conference.

Rehabtool.com www.rehabtool.com
Rehabtool.com offers a variety of high-tech assistive and adaptive technology products, augmentative communication devices, computer access equipment, multilingual speech synthesis and voice recognition software. They also offer virtual on-screen keyboards, voice-enabled

Continued on next page

Table 4.4 (continued)

communication boards, as well as cognitive rehabilitation tools adapted to the special needs of the disabled. Information on upcoming training and conferences are available on the site as well.

Vision Connection www.visionconnection.org
VisionConnection is an accessible, interactive Internet portal for people who are partially sighted or blind, professionals, families, or people looking for the latest information on vision impairment, prevention, and rehabilitation. The site also contains information about the newest advances in assistive technology, upcoming technology events, accessible Web sites and more. The site has accessibility options built in to allow people with low vision to access the information on the site more easily.

Assistive Technology Information and Resources

Assistive technology information and resources are also expanding at great rates and those involved with transitioning students with disabilities from high school to postsecondary education or the world of work must try to keep abreast with this information to be as effective as possible when transition planning. In order to do this, people must try to educate themselves about assistive technology. Table 4.5 contains some useful web resources to help teachers, parents, and other professionals learn more about AT information and resources.

Table 4.5
Assistive Technology Information and Resources

Assistivetech.net http://www.assistivetech.net
Assistivetech.net is a resource for assistive technology and has links to a variety of AT and disability-related information. The site contains a searchable database of AT is designed to target solutions, determine costs, and link people to vendors that sell products. The website also includes links to online resources on disability-related topics, discussion lists, and chat rooms for people who need ideas on how to solve AT problems.

ATA http://www.ataccess.org
The Alliance for Technology Access (ATA) is a network of community-based resource centers, developers, vendors, and associates dedicated to providing information and support services to children and adults with disabilities, and increasing their use of standard, assistive, and information technologies. This website contains various AT and AT-related resources and information for people with disabilities, educators, families, and vendors. There are also descriptions of ATA's initiatives, publications, and projects related to AT.

AT Network http://www.atnet.org/
The AT Network website provides a myriad of resources in the areas of advocacy, AT legislation, AT information, and other topics related to education and AT. They also have an AT

Continued on next page

Table 4.5 (continued)

journal and AT directory that can be accessed through this website. The site could be beneficial for parents, teachers, and people with disabilities who are looking for background information on AT, answers to specific questions, and help with accessing AT that they need.

Closing the Gap http://www.closingthegap.com
Closing The Gap, Inc. is an organization that focuses on computer technology for people with special needs through its bi-monthly newspaper, annual international conference, and extensive website. The website contains a resource directory which has information about software, hardware, producers, organizations, and other AT. There is also a "Solutions" section on the website that includes articles and products for different disability areas and needs. Information on their annual conference is also included.

DREAMMS for Kids http://www.dreamms.org
The DREAMMS for Kids, Inc. website contains information for parents, professionals, and people with disabilities on state AT organizations, as well as links to information on AT and disability-related topics. The links include governmental websites, university websites, and other websites that contain AT devices and AT-related information. There is also a newsletter entitled "Directions" that can be accessed through the website.

Family Guide to Assistive Technology www.pluk.org/AT1.html#2
The Family Guide to Assistive Technology is an on-line resource for families of individuals with disabilities. This guide includes information for families on making AT decisions, funding AT, AT in educational settings, and advocating for AT, as well as many forms and other resources that the families can use related to those topics.

Illinois Assistive Technology Project http://www.iltech.org
The TechConnect website is part of the Illinois Assistive Technology Project which includes articles on topics related to AT as well as a list of the devices available through their lending library for teachers, parents, and students to use. The site also contains a list of links and publications that serve as resources for people needing information on AT selection, funding, and advocacy.

Worksupport.com www.worksupport.com
The Worksupport.com website contains information and resources regarding work and disability issues. The site includes articles, on-line training opportunities, products, answers to frequently asked questions, and other resources for people with disabilities in the workforce.

Assistive Technology Training and Resources

In order to learn more about assistive technology and resources individuals must be proactive and get involved with their own learning. This education will allow those who participate to be more involved in the transition planning process regarding assistive technology. One way to do this is to attend conferences and training that emphasizes assistive technology. Table 4.6 contains some useful web resources to help teachers, parents, and other professionals learn more about AT training and resources.

Table 4.6
Assistive Technology Training and Resources

PAT http://www.pat.org
The Partnerships in Assistive Technology website contains information about its upcoming 2004 Assistive Technology Expo, as well as other AT training opportunities throughout North Carolina. The site includes information about the PAT's current projects, the North Carolina Assistive Technology Consortium, and other assistive technology resources in North Carolina. The site has a section called "Exchange Post" where people can place ads to sell AT devices that others can purchase through the site.

RESNA http://www.resna.org
The RESNA website offers a variety of information related to AT and AT advocacy. There is information about their annual conference, including the workshops available, professional development opportunities in the area of AT, and a job bank for AT-related jobs included on the site. In addition, descriptions and resources related to their Alternative Financing and Technical Assistance projects are contained in this site.

Assistive Technology Research

Teachers, parents, and other professionals must also learn to investigate the effectiveness of assistive technologies. When teams are considering the use of AT to aid students with disabilities transition from high school to postsecondary education or the world of work they should look to see what type of research support the AT has. They should also investigate how easily the research can be translated into practice and how feasible the AT under consideration fits with the needs and abilities of the student. Table 4.7 contains some useful web resources to help teachers, parents, and other professionals learn more about AT research.

Table 4.7
Assistive Technology Research

NATRI http://natri.uky.edu/
The National Assistive Technology Research Institute (NATRI) conducts AT research, translates theory and research into AT practice, and provides resources for improving the delivery of AT services. The website contains articles, reports, and information on various topics related to AT, as well as AT device videos and other on-line resources. Three on-line surveys related to NATRI research projects are available on the website for people to give input on AT use and needs.

Continued on next page

Table 4.7 (continued)

TransCen, Inc. http://www.transcen.org
TransCen, Inc. is a nonprofit organization dedicated to improving educational and employment outcomes for people with disabilities. The associates at TransCen, Inc. have developed, implemented, and researched innovations regarding school-to-adult life transition and career development for people with disabilities.

FINAL THOUGHTS

Planning the transition from high school to postsecondary education or the world of work for students with disabilities is an essential and critical aspect of our job. Involving assistive technology in this process should be considered as a viable strategy for all students. The most important thing to keep in mind while considering the use of AT devices and services in the transition process is the individual needs of the student. What one student needs to be successful can be totally different than what another student might need. Devices for students can range from no-tech devices to low-tech devices to high-tech devices. It is suggested that a technology continuum be implemented where teams begin with possible no-tech devices and work their way up the continuum until an appropriate assistive technology is chosen. It is important to utilize the expertise and ideas of all members of the IEP team, especially those of the student and the family. Knowing what services a school district is responsible for providing as well as using a model such as the SETT Framework will aid the decision makers in this process. This will also make the evaluation and selection process run more smoothly and be more effective. The goal of the whole transition process is to ensure that the student is prepared for "real life" after graduation, no matter what career path he or she chooses to take. Planning for AT is just a piece of that puzzle that could allow students to reach the goals that they have set out for themselves and it is our job as educators to involve them and their parents as well as other professionals in this process.

Chapter 5

PLANNING AND DEVELOPING STUDENT-FOCUSED INDIVIDUALIZED TRANSITION PLANS

Doug, a Caucasian male, is 14 years old and is currently a freshman in high school. He has been diagnosed with Asperger's syndrome with specific deficiencies in *social* and *communication skills*. Mentally, Doug has a normal intelligence and has standard *language development* compared to students who have classical *autism*. Academically, he does well in most of his classes; however, he tends to experience poor communication skills, obsessive or repetitive routines, and physical clumsiness which affect his social standing in his classes. When working independently, he is very successful, but he has more problems when he is required to work in a group setting. In a group, he has difficulty communicating his thoughts and ideas and frequently gets off-task doing some repetitive routine. Some students do not want to work with him because of his behaviors. Doug's case manager, Ms. Conway, is concerned about him getting the vocational skills training and transition plan that he needs to be successful after graduation. She wants to include Doug and his parents in the planning and development of his IEP and ITP as well as choices and available services, but she also does not want to end up doing all of the work alone.

How can Ms. Conway get Doug's parents to fully participate in the IEP and ITP processes? How can Ms. Conway make Doug more accountable for his own learning and behaviors through proper transition planning? This chapter responds to these critical questions.

INDIVIDUALIZING STUDENTS' NEEDS

When transitioning students with disabilities, general and special educators and other service providers must assess their overall needs. In addition, these professionals must teach them to assess their own needs. It has been found that successful people assess their needs, determine their goals, plan their actions, monitor their performance, and make any needed adjustments (Mithaug, Martin, & Agran, 1987). Basically, successful people assess their own strengths and weaknesses and use that information to help them to be successful in different situations throughout their lives. Unfortunately, students with disabilities frequently do not understand their disability, strengths, and needs because the adults in their lives often feel compelled to over protect them (Jones, 2006). After exiting school, many former special education students cannot plan their future, remain unemployed or underemployed, and experience a quality of life remarkably different from their nondisabled peers (Hasazi, Gordon, & Roe, 1985; McNair & Rusch, 1990; Mithaug, Horiuchi, & Fanning, 1985). For example, many students may be limited in their opportunities to perform odd jobs around their neighborhoods, assist with family chores, and engage in other activities that allow them to acquire basic vocational skills and good work habits (Clark & Kolstoe, 1995).

Although IDEA dictates that comprehensive transition services need not be addressed until the student is 16, there is little justification for waiting until then to begin this conversation, particularly given a context of the individualized education program (IEP) as a strategic transition plan. Age 14 typically signals entry into high school, and students and families need to develop an awareness of graduation requirements and diploma options as soon as possible. To individualize and plan ITPs, questions such as the following might be posed in the transition dialogue:

- What are the student's long-term goals?
- How can these goals be accomplished within the typical four years of high school?
- How will this experience prepare the student to live and work in the community or attend college?
- What objectives, activities, or special education supports and services are needed this year to help progress toward these goals?

• What school or community resources are needed to address any at-risk behaviors that are present?

Clearly, these are critical questions that deserve the attention of general and special educators. IEP annual goals and services can then be developed both in response to this dialogue and in anticipation of service needs for future years (deFur, 2003).

EMPOWERING STUDENTS IN THE TRANSITION PROCESS

For students to become involved in the transition process, they must be empowered. They must be taught about their own disability and what they are capable of doing presently and in the future. There are four premises underlying the process toward student empowerment. The first premise is that students with disabilities are able to gain knowledge about their abilities, their IEPs, the IEP process, and why they receive services (Jones, 2006). Here, students must understand what their disability means and can talk about it to others. They must be encouraged to become comfortable stating what they need and what they do not need (Warger & Burnette, 2000). Second, no student is too young to learn about himself or herself and to become involved in decision making about his/her education (Jones, 2006). Third, student empowerment promotes learning as students are encouraged to engage in inquiry, develop leadership skills, and make decisions that affect their own lives. Fourth, student empowerment is contagious (Jones, 2006). The more they are involved and empowered, the more they will become involved in the process. Professionals who empower students must be themselves empowered. They must work with parents to form a solid transition foundation. Clearly, the successful employment of adults with disabilities has been attributed to career choices and self-survival skills (Gerber, Ginsberg, & Reiff, 1992).

Skills identified for effective job performance or "workplace know-how" include basic skills, thinking skills, and personal qualities such as responsibility, integrity, and honesty. Individuals must also be able to use resources, acquire information, work with others, understand systems, and use technology (Sarkees-Wircenski & Wircenski, 1994). These skills must be considered when planning a student's future. For the most part, when efforts to plan the future have been made, the foci must be daily and community living skills (Sitlington, 1996). In order to prepare young people for life after high school, community or daily living skills instruction must begin early in their school careers. In preschool and kindergarten, children must begin to learn the importance of dressing one's self, cleaning up one's mess, having the responsibility of a "job" in class, and going on field trips. All life skills must be taught within an academic situation. Unfortunately, after kindergarten, efforts are rarely made to teach daily living skills. As a result, people forget skills that will help them to survive life's journeys. Some life skills are taught directly, whereas others are imitated and learned, but many are taken for granted because someone else is supposed to take the responsibility for doing the task. It is important to teach life skills throughout the student's school experience, regardless of the student's age or grade. Students cannot be empowered until educational programs that are designed to help them are implemented.

DEVELOPING SELF-DETERMINATION SKILLS IN TRANSITIONAL PROGRAMS

Self-determined people know how to choose. They know what they want and use their self-advocacy skills to get it. From an awareness of personal needs, self-determined individuals choose goals and persistently pursue those goals; this involves asserting their presence, making their needs known, evaluating progress toward meeting their goals, adjusting their performance, and creating unique approaches to solve problems (Agran, Martin, & Mithaug, 1989). Broadly defined, self-determination is a person's freedom to make decisions independently (Schloss, Alper, & Jayne, 1994). Making choices about work, education, and independent living are examples of self-determining behaviors. Ludi and Martin (1995) acknowledged that self-determination may have differing meanings based on cultural identity and type of disability, but concluded that "culture itself does not alter the meaning of self-determination, but it is likely to change some of the characteristics developed and the manner in which that development takes place" (p.165).

Experiences that students have frequently impact their self-determination abilities. Teachers and other professionals involved in the transition process must examine not only the types of high school experiences most likely to foster self-determination, but the processes by which students' self-determination interacts with high school experiences and the variation in their experiences (Eisenman, 2001). Students, when appropriate, must be key players in the transition process and must make plans of action that will help them achieve their goals and desires. It is important to take advantage of what students know about and value in themselves (Field, Hoffman, & Spezia, 1998). To be successful, students must take long-term goals and break them into a series of short-term goals that build upon each other to lead them towards success. Students must learn that they have choices to make and that all choices have consequences. With that in mind, students must know they are responsible for their own actions and choices. This should, however, be a gradual process where the student is guided at first with his/her responsibility by the professional, teacher, and/or parent; and gradually, the student can assume his/her own responsibility. Getting students to predict or think of potential negative effects of certain choices is a goal that allows students to think about all options and outcomes before making a decision that will, hopefully, be as positive and beneficial as possible.

Although many teachers and other professionals agree that it is important to teach self-determination, a relatively low percentage of special education teachers actually implement a self determination program or include goals and objectives related to self-determination on student IEPS (Grigal, Neubert, Moon, & Graham, 2003; Wehmeyer, Agran, & Hughes, 2000). The development of self-determination competencies challenges students to become actively involved in the IEP planning process, yet it is not known how comfortable students and families are with these concepts (Miner & Bates, 1997). Ultimately, self-determination and overall student empowerment improve the quality of students' adult lives. Increasing students' self-determination may increase their success in moving from high school to adult living (Wehmeyer, 1995). In their work, Wehmeyer and Schwartz (1997) found that (a) self-determined adolescents with cognitive disabilities leave school to have more positive adult outcomes than do their peers with cognitive disabilities who are less self-determined, and (b) adults with cognitive disabilities who are self-determined experience a higher quality of life.

IEP DEVELOPMENT IN THE TRANSITION PROCESS

The IEP is the primary planning document in special education designed to individualize goals and instruction and coordinate services needed to complete those goals for students with special needs at all age levels. The mandated statement of transition by IDEA needs to be included in the IEPs of all students ages 16 and over (age 14 when appropriate). The IEP present level of educational performance forms the student biographical foundation from which all other IEP decisions are made. Goals, objectives, benchmarks, accommodations, modifications, supplementary aids, extended school year, participation with nondisabled peers, and services must emanate from this documented baseline. There should be a direct relationship between the student transition needs, interests, and preferences identified in the present level of educational performance and all other components in the IEP (deFur, 2003). By law, families need to be told of the time, location, and purpose of the IEP meeting, but the meeting itself can be arranged to be more family and student-friendly by (a) sending home premeeting planning tools or an agenda so families and students can come prepared to share their ideas; (b) beginning the meeting with a clear orientation to the process and the goals of the meeting and how decisions will be made; (c) paying sincere attention to and using family and student input; (d) providing structured opportunities for questions and answers; (e) adopting the value that students are the central agents in their transition planning; and (f) offering clear opportunities for shared leadership within the meeting. In the end, IEP teams should consider the timing and physical setting of the meeting and try to ensure that these do not conflict with family employment and caretaking needs (deFur, 2003).

Collett-Ligenberg (1998) and Krom and Prater (1993) argued that the transition development process must be comprehensive. In their study, they found that the IEPs of secondary special education students almost exclusively focused on academics with no obvious links between goals, objectives, and transition outcomes. In addition, little can be found in the research that suggests that IEPs address adult living objectives related to leisure and recreation. This must change and be a priority to include in this process. During IEP/ITP meetings, parents and students may vary in their level of comfort in accepting a central planning role, especially if they view educators as having higher status. This will likely influence the scope of their participation, as well as their expectations of one another. Parents may be uncomfortable allowing their child to play a leadership role in a meeting of adults and professionals (Miner & Bates, 1997). Equal status of IEP/ITP team members means that the input of each is a significant driving force behind final decisions including parents. If parents come from cultures that value hierarchical structure, the idea that they or their children have the right and responsibility to advocate for their needs may be foreign to them (Kalyanpur & Harry, 1999). As a result, students must be invited to attend their IEP/ITP meetings if the purpose of the meeting will be to consider their transition service needs (Warger & Burnette, 2000).

In addition to teaching students about their disabilities, students benefit greatly by being shown copies of their IEPs followed by explanations of their personal present levels of performance, goals, objectives, and specially designed instructional needs (Jones, 2006). To nurture a student's involvement in the IEP process, students should be taught to determine their own future IEP goals and encouraged to identify what they think is the most important goal. By actually engaging students in designing their own personal IEP goals, students will become empowered members in the IEP process. One component of facilitating student empowerment that is invaluable is vision planning. It is particularly motivating for students to think about and actually articulating their hopes and dreams for the future (see Jones, 2006). Another highly beneficial activity could be guiding students in monitoring progress toward the achievement of specific goals and objectives. However, before students can be expected to participate in their IEP meetings, time needs to be spent preparing IEP participants. There are two parts to this preparation process. The first is to prepare the student to participate in his IEP meeting (Jones, 2006). Aside from role-playing, a second key feature for preparing students to participate in their IEP meetings is that they need to dictate how involved they plan to become in the IEP process (Jones, 2006). Time should be scheduled for students to develop skills related to IEP participation on a regular basis. General and special education teachers must believe self-determination, planning, and self-advocacy skills are priorities (Warger & Burnette, 2000). As a result, preteaching, role playing, videotaping, and providing specific feedback on the social skills required and the decision-making structure of IEP transition meetings must take place to increase student involvement in the process (deFur, 2003).

Within all societies, values that guide social interaction, communication, and survival are points on a continuum of individuality and collectivity. Individualism and self-reliance are distinct cultural values relative to self-determination that may or may not be shared by all members of this diverse nation (Harry, Rueda, & Kalyanpur, 1999). Elements of transition planning and self-determination, such as moving into an independent residence or leaving home to pursue postsecondary educational opportunities, are influenced by this orientation. Students need transition plans to better prepare them for the future and to guide teachers to properly train them to be successful when they leave the school system for postschool experiences. Since it is mandated for students with disabilities, transition plans need to be written to also reflect multicultural differences. Although Rusch and Phelps (1987) suggested that transition planning and services are an effective way of improving the postschool outcomes of youths with disabilities, general and special educators need to be careful that they make transition plans for future careers that are in consonance with individuals' cultures, values, and aspirations. They need to allow multicultural learners with disabilities every opportunity to work towards and achieve career goals whenever possible. Persons involved in transition planning should not allow stereotypical views of culturally diverse groups or preconceived notions of student abilities to influence them. Clearly, in IEP/ITP plannings, it is critical to make (a) student participation crucial, (b) families involved in the transition process, (c) transition efforts to start early, (d) transition planning sensitive to cultural factors, (e) transition planning comprehensive, (f) transition planning to reflect students' strengths and needs, and (g) differences of opinion clear (Moery, 1993). Each transition plan therefore must reflect the abilities and stated needs and preferences of a particular student and not what someone else thinks the person should do or what the school's limited options offer (see Moery, 1993). The involvement of parents and guardians in the transition planning process empowers them to serve as both advocates and service coordinators for their adolescent with special needs (Patton & Browder, 1988). Through the ITP process, parents, students, school officials, and adult service providers can come to an agreement regarding the direction of the transition plan. All parties involved in the process must clearly identify their goals and values with respect to the student's future. This helps to clarify differences in goals early in the planning process and allows for resolution of those differences.

PROVIDING TRANSITION SERVICES

There are program elements that best support transitional service needs of school-age students (Cobb & Hasazi, 1987). These elements include an individualized transitional plan, integration within secondary vocational education programs, paid work experiences, a job-seeking skills curriculum, flexible staffing patterns, active parent/consumer involvement, follow-up surveys of special education graduates, and data transfer and management across school and adult services agencies. It is always necessary to (a) instruct students on job-seeking skills, (b) give them curriculum support for part-time jobs both during the summer and the school year, and (c) give support to regular vocational education teachers. To do these, general and special educators will need to have flexible staffing arrangements to provide regionally based consultation with vocational educators, job site training, and support for after-school job-seeking education programs.

It is important for students with disabilities to receive career counseling and participate in career-development programs during secondary school. These programs help students to select careers that will utilize strengths and de-emphasize weaknesses and attain employment by teaching them skills in filling out application forms and interviewing for employment. They may also help students to handle problems that arise on the job, including problems with interpersonal skills and anger control (Hutchinson, 1995). Career counseling group interventions using cognitive instruction have been recommended for youth with disabilities. In cognitive instruction, counselors and teachers provide clear explanations and models of behaviors and thinking that students may not be able to develop spontaneously. Students practice with peers in pairs and small groups, adapting problem-solving approaches and explanations of the teacher to develop their own understanding (Englert, Tarrant, & Mariage, 1992).

During the transition process, students may be exposed to other options. Some students may need employment assistance on only a short-term or temporary basis; others may require long-term services provided by a supported employment agency for the entire duration of their employment. Some students may require only information and guidance in how to acquire assistive technology or other types of support; others may need ongoing, continuous supervision and assistance in basic activities of daily living (Sarkees-Wircenski & Wircenski, 1994). For some students, community-based instruction may be an option. Some examples of community-based activities include comparison shopping for everything (e.g., food, clothes, and cars); depositing weekend babysitting or lawn-mowing money in a savings account in a bank; preparing lunch for the class within a budget while reflecting nutritional guidelines and taking into consideration the group's likes and dislikes; and learning how to ride public transportation using transfers to and from school, work, and shopping areas. When instruction takes place in the community, students must be adequately prepared prior to leaving campus (e.g., permissions are sought, safety instructions given, and adequate insurance coverage obtained). It is important for community sites to be prepared for instruction to take place at their location (e.g., notification of visit sent to site manager, with an explanation of the purpose of the visit; insurance of adequate supervision of the students at the site). In the end, an evaluation of each student's performance of tasks in the community is essential (Moery, 1993).

In the transition process, collaboration, consultation, and cooperation are keys to adequate programming. Collaboration among the school, the local education agency, and adult service providers frequently are necessary to promote effective transition planning (Patton & Browder, 1988). According to Patton and Browder, four steps can facilitate interagency cooperation. First, the development of interagency agreements that formalize the collaborative process would enable parents and students to coordinate services effectively. Second, the loosening of organizational and procedural constraints would facilitate the provision of necessary services from different agencies. Third, interagency meetings to negotiate the scope, parameters, responsibilities, and funding configurations for persons with disabilities would provide more effective service delivery. Finally, an agreement on the method for implementing collaborative agreements would put at the forefront the needs of the client rather than the needs of the agencies.

FINAL THOUGHTS

When developing IEPs and ITPs, it is crucial that general and special education teachers and other professionals involve parents and the students themselves in this process. We must consider the needs of the students when creating transition documents and plans. Developing self-determination skills in students is one way to help promote their involvement in the transition process as well as on-going opportunities to communicate their wants and needs. We must realize that students with disabilities must be made accountable for their actions and decisions and that their choices can have a lasting impression on them and their future lives and careers. Since every student with a disability has an IEP and is part of the special education system, it would seem appropriate for special educators to collect information on their former students, as vocational educators have done for their students, since the 1976 Amendments to the Vocational Education Act. Data regarding the relationship of high school education and training experiences are critical to knowing how effective a program and process is. It is very important to know how appropriate the curriculum and experiences offered during high school are for all students with disabilities.

Chapter 6

COLLABORATING WITH FAMILIES IN THE TRANSITION PROCESS

Mr. and Mrs. Lopez are apprehensive about participating in the transition planning meeting for their son, Jose, who has a hearing impairment. Jose is a freshman in high school, and his case manager, Ms. Smith, is concerned about him getting the vocational skills training that he needs to be successful after graduation. Mr. and Mrs. Lopez have not been very involved in the IEP meetings for Jose in the past because they have felt that teachers and professionals knew best how to help their son. Understandably, Spanish is their first language, and Mrs. Lopez does not speak much English. As a result, they have difficulty understanding other members of the transition planning team during meetings.

How might Ms. Smith help Mr. and Mrs. Lopez to feel like active members of the team, and become more involved in the transition planning process? Surely, some skills are needed. This chapter responds to this critical question. Before children even walk into a classroom, be it pre-school or kindergarten, they have been with the most influential, long-lasting teacher in their lives: a parent. Parents are a child's first teacher whose lessons undoubtedly continue throughout life. Therefore, it should not be surprising for educational policies and laws to be designed with the inclusion of family members in decision-making processes regarding placement and, in this case, a plan for the child's future adult life. By the time students with disabilities reach the age at which transition planning is appropriate and mandated by law, they might have come in contact with approximately 10 different teachers. It is the parent, however, who has been continuously with the student. Clearly, parents hold information most vital to educators during this time in their children's lives. Strengths, weaknesses, likes, dislikes, dreams, and hobbies are all aspects of a young person's life which need to be discussed and documented to design an appropriate transition plan which will benefit him/her in the future. To come together in a productive teaming situation, educators must learn to appreciate the parents' role as teachers, understand the family structure, and develop ways to effectively communicate to ensure success for the student.

UNDERSTANDING FAMILY INVOLVEMENT

The teenage years can be a stressful time in any family's life, and this can be certainly elevated with the presence of a disability. Ward, Mallett, Heslop, and Simons (2003) reported that parents were dissatisfied with the transition process because of a lack of information being provided to them. Parents felt unprepared to assist their adolescents in making decisions which could affect their futures. Earlier, Goupil, Tasse, Garcin, and Dore (2002) noted that parents' concerns for their children include areas of social life, safety, future employment, residential services, and personal autonomy. Yet, again, parents had little knowledge of work, leisure, and community services which could be available for their sons and daughters. This lack of information is most unfortunate especially when the parent has "intimate and important knowledge of the medical history of the child and his or her daily routines, habits, likes and dislikes, behaviors, and family needs, and sees the child within his or her natural context" (Lytle & Bordin, 2001, p. 41). deFur, Todd-Allen, and Getzel (2003) identified several problems of parental participation and apprehension during transition planning. First and foremost, families from low socioeconomic status may be viewed by professionals as being naïve about the education and best placements for their children. Service providers sometimes feel that their opinions are best and refuse to share information with families. In addition, school and special education practices and policies may develop barriers to more active parental roles. Professionals often use jargon and act comfortable with one another, often leaving parents out of conversations.

Lytle and Bordin (2001) revealed that school professionals often work closely together all year, possibly even for many years, whereas parents are not part of this daily interaction. Parents are often left out of the joking, chatting, and basic camaraderie between professionals. For these reasons, professionals must take the time to foster an inviting environment for parental participation and membership to the team (Lytle & Bordin, 2001). Furthermore, parental perceptions of their equity as team members may be lessened due to the structure of meetings that solely focus on student weaknesses. Unfortunately, by the time transition planning takes place, parents may have had years of experience in IEP meetings which have been plagued by such barriers. As Lytle and Bordin noted, when viewing a child, professionals have been trained to be objective, whereas parents tend to be more subjective. This often causes a clash between both points of view. However, if both parents and professionals can recognize and accept the others' perspectives, feelings of teamwork and an opportunity for the creation of a holistic view of the child can be developed. This common ground for both professionals and parents is the key to find what is best for families and students with disabilities. To assist parents in the transition process, educators and service providers must recognize that parents experience feelings of dread when talking about their child's adult life (Goupil et al., 2002). Therefore, it is increasingly important for professionals to be sensitive to families' individual needs and try to appreciate that each child is one key player in a unique family structure (Pruitt, Wandry, & Hollums, 1998). According to Pruitt and colleagues, professionals need to realize that every family is different, and therefore, should get to know each family to appreciate their point of view. In addition, professionals should not ask too much of parents since they have their own logistical and time constraints.

In today's multicultural society, professionals should possess knowledge of cultural differences and ways in which this may effect family interaction with the school. As Greene (1996) defined, cultural behaviors include, but are "not limited to institutions, language, values, religion, symbols, ideals, habits of thinking, artistic expressions, and patterns of social and interpersonal relationships" (p. 26). He added that cultural beliefs and practices exist on a continuum. Therefore, no two families, even from similar cultural backgrounds, are likely to function exactly the same way. Members of IEP/transition teams need to be aware of various cultural and social factors in order to interact in appropriate, rather than stereotypical ways. Any goal of a transition plan is to start career education early and to take full advantage of each student's strengths and dreams. "Increasing cultural awareness and sensitivity to differences is imperative for successful transition planning" (Boone, 1992, p. 54). Greene (1996) listed several ways in which professionals can become more acquainted with families from diverse backgrounds prior to team meetings. First, it is important for professionals to know what language is spoken in the home, and by whom. This may prevent frustration for both parties in current and future communications. In addition to language, professionals should assess the literacy of the family to ensure that all written communication can be understood. Ideas regarding the family's views toward the adolescent's independence, as well as residential and employment goals should be obtained. Other information regarding knowledge of legal rights and parental views regarding the child's disability should provide professionals with more information to increase parental satisfaction of the transition process.

EFFECTIVE COMMUNICATION IN THE TRANSITION PROCESS

To ultimately overcome barriers and introduce parents into a process in which they are equal members, professionals must practice effective communication strategies among themselves and the parents with whom they work. In their study, Ward et al. (2003) noted that parents perceived a mismatch in what they wanted their children's transition plans to include and what the parents received. To prevent such confusion in expectations, professionals must make efficient use of their communicative strategies. Because the IEP/transition process is the one mandated interaction between school and family, meetings should foster positive home-school relations (Pruitt et al., 1998). This collaborative relationship will not just appear, nor will it develop overnight. Strong collaborative, supportive relationships between parents and professionals are developed over time with frequent, effective, and interactive communication between all parties (Greene, 1996; Salembier & Furney, 1997). Since relationships are rarely formed at a high-stress meeting, it should not be shocking that parents find it easier to participate when relationships have been established prior to transition planning (see Salembier & Furney). Over time, professionals and parents must build their relationship on shared responsibility and mutual trust (deFur et al., 2003; Salembier & Furney, 1997) and common goals that reflect the student's best interest (Pruitt et al., 1998).

Professionals can improve communication and interaction with parents exponentially by following some simple steps to establish constant, open dialogue with the home. Salembier and Furney (1997) indicated that enhancing communication between parents and professionals includes not only shared goals for students but parents being knowledgeable regarding the IEP/transition process, their legal rights and responsibilities, and information regarding various community services. Establishing a good relationship early with parents is essential. Newsletters sent home, invitations to parents to participate in the classroom or school, and phone calls home which update parents on classroom progress and stress positive aspects of the student can be ways in which teachers reach out to parents (Pruitt et al., 1998). See Table 6.1 for ways to build rapport with families. When communication occurs more often in a relaxed atmosphere and a relationship has been established between professionals and parents, transition planning and key points of contention can be less stressful for all involved. Clearly, a personal rather than a bureaucratic relationship during transitioning is most desirable (deFur, 2003).

EMPOWERING PARENTS DURING THE TRANSITION PROCESS

A common theme across the literature is that parents prefer to be asked their opinions, not ultimately told what to do be professionals during the transition plan (e.g., deFur et al., 2001; Pruitt et al., 1998). More often than not, parents' needs for information in assisting their sons and daughters in decision-making processes are not recognized by professionals (Ward et al., 2003). When parents are asked, rather than given information, feelings of helplessness that are often felt by parents within the process can be reduced. Being asked for opinions and suggestions is also a way for parents to feel they are making meaningful contributions to the team and to their child's welfare. deFur & Patton (1999) reiterated that many parents often become service coor-

Table 6.1
Ideas for Improving Parent-School Relationships

Beginning of the School Year	• Introduce yourself as the case manager/teacher and provide contact information (Phone # & e-mail address) • Send home a syllabus or a parent letter outlining your expectations for the students in your classroom • Send newsletters home with class activities/topics regularly • Call or e-mail parents regularly to share student progress reports (positive and negative)
Throughout the School Year	• Ask for parent input whenever needed (i.e., discipline issues, concerns with academic progress, etc.) • Invite parents to participate in classroom activities and projects • Invite the parents to volunteer at the school
Prior to/After IEP Meetings	• Inform parents of their legal rights in the IEP/ transition process • Ask for parent input on student progress and concerns, as well as possible goals/objectives • Inform parents of the available community services related to their student's particular needs

dinators for their children after graduation. Not asking for their input would be disastrous. Ward and associates noted that it would be helpful for parents to have the advice and guidance of professionals during transition planning and be told key persons who would be attending meetings, with information regarding those individuals' responsibilities. As Ward et al. agreed, having available one person or coordinator who has access to all necessary literature and services and "who will guide parents through the minefield of obstacles put in the way while trying to seek positive help" is critical (p. 136). Regardless, professionals who make a difference readily share information concerning community resources, progress, and opportunities for students often before parents can ask for them during the transition process. Finally, it is important to understand that parents recognize professionals who show special care for student and family needs. This includes parents' need to celebrate their children's strengths with the professional, as well as hear encouragement among team members.

Professionals must be cognizant of various ways in which parents, especially those from ethnically diverse groups may communicate. Some cultural groups may rely more heavily upon nonverbal communication, whereas others depend heavily upon what is said (Boone, 1992). Boone stated that variations in communication styles should not be viewed by professionals as deficiencies. Differences in communication styles include nonverbal cues (e.g., facial expressions, gestures, and tone), eye gazing or eye contact, and conversational turn-taking. Again, having knowledge of each family's mode of communication and preferences before sitting down to IEP/transition meetings would greatly increase the effectiveness of the team, and in the long run, empowers the parents. As Lytle and Bordin (2001) indicated, sharing information both verbally and in written form does not make for a successful meeting between parents and professionals; nonverbal communication should be equally monitored. Professionals need to be aware of their own gestures, expressions, and body positions to ensure positive lines of communication are kept open. Subtle, nonverbal signs can be as powerful as the verbal message professionals are trying to get across. Someone sitting forward, smiling, and making open gestures is more likely to be greeted positively by a parent than one who is sitting back with arms crossed, sipping coffee, and rolling his/her eyes.

With advances in technology, most school and service providers now have access to video recording devices. Alberto, Mechling, Taber, and Thompson (1995) suggested various ways in which video recording devices can be utilized during the transition planning process to increase the communication and collaboration between parents and professionals. For classroom teachers, videotapes of students would be a way to show parents the behavioral and vocational expectations within a training site. For students, creating video resumes would be a way to demonstrate to parents and employers success at various work-related skills. At a planning meeting, video of a student in various work situations would be a powerful tool in deciding skills and strategies which may need to be enhanced. See Table 6.2 for a checklist of strategies that professionals should be mindful of when working with families through the transition process.

Table 6.2
Strategies for Working with Parents During the Transition Planning Process

Communication	• Avoid using jargon and acronyms that the parents may not know or understand • Be aware of the parents' nonverbal cues, as well as the non-verbal cues that you may be sending to them • Be aware of the parents' most comfortable mode of communication and arrange for interpreters as needed • Follow up with parents after the meeting with any additional information that was obtained • Use effective listening and communication skills with the parents during the meeting, to ensure that they feel their opinions/suggestions are being heard
Collaboration	• Give parents the names and contact information for one or two professionals that can answer the parents' questions and be a source of information for them • Assist the parents in making contacts with various community resources • Ensure that the parents feel like an active part of the team and decision-making process
Information	• Ask parents for information/opinions about their child prior to the transition planning meeting • Listen to and consider parent suggestions at the meeting • Use videotapes of the student in the classroom to show student progress • Use videotaped examples of vocational training sites and/or selected careers to help determine a student's need for assistance in these settings

ECOURAGING FAMILY PARTICIPATION IN TRANSITION PLANNING

The golden rule of transition planning is this: Attendance does not equal participation (deFur et al., 2001) when it comes to families working in the transition process. Equality and equity in the transition team is something that does not just happen; it is worked at by all members of the team before, during, and after actual meetings take place. Parents often need both professionals' information and social support to reduce stress and increase their own knowledge and understanding of educational practices (Lytle & Bordin, 2001).

Planning for Transition Meetings

Before IEP/transition meetings occur, parent-professional communication and a working relationship built on trust and honesty must be established. Working at transition while not being familiar with each other is likely to cause undue stress and, as Lytle and Bordin (2001) pointed out, becomes an unlikely situation for developing a strong team relationship. Parent satisfaction can be increased by teachers who demonstrate flexibility and who support and encourage students, as well as the family (Ward et al., 2003). In addition, parent confidence can be increased in the transition process when professionals demonstrate dedication and have their adolescents' best interest at heart (see Ward et al.). To help parents focus and understand the transition process, Hutchins and Renzaglia (1998) presented a number of questions for professionals to ask to help stimulate family discussion (see Table 6.3 below). Parents can provide information regarding the student's current responsibilities at home and how he/she spends free time. Topics such as anticipated residential needs, number of hours during the work week, and family resources can be addressed by the parents. By asking such questions, not only are professionals establishing a guideline for parental expectations but also gaining rapport with the family.

Table 6.3
Focus Questions for Parents

- What responsibilities does your student currently have at home?
- Which of those responsibilities, if any, does your student need the most help with?
- How does your student usually spend his/her free time?
- What do you see as your student's strengths?
- What are you most concerned with about your student?
- In which possible careers has your student expressed interest?
- What are your hopes for your student after high school?
- What plans have you and/or your student made for education/work after high school?

If your student has a job:
- How many hours per week does he/she work?
- What skills are involved in that job?
- What parts of his/her job are the most difficult for him/her?

As the literature reveals, role clarity during transition planning is a must (Thompson, Fulk, & Piercy, 2000; Wehmeyer & Sands, 1998). "Active participation can only occur when parents and students have the skills and knowledge needed to participate" (Thompson et al., 2000, p. 21). To assist in identifying roles, professionals must be prepared to make suggestions to parents and students alike on how to increase their participation by respecting their input (Lytle & Bordin, 2001). Additionally, professionals need to realize that not all families will have the same amount of participation. As a result, they should provide families with choices in levels of comfortable participation. Boone (1992) stated that it would be wise for professionals to "affirm parent's right to choose passive participation without labeling them as uncaring" (p. 218). It is the duty of professionals to ensure that minimal participation is by choice, not due to parents' lack of information or level of preparedness (Boone, 1992).

Responding to Cultural Diversity

Greene (1996) provided an outline for professionals who are working with families from culturally diverse backgrounds. The proposed strategies are given to increase the ways in which professionals can increase their cultural sensitivities. It is important for parents to understand that the child is not just a case number. Professionals should avoid using stigmatizing labels or vocabulary which could be viewed by parents as insulting. They should make attempts to see and appreciate the child through the eyes of the parents and other family members. Table 6.4 below lists some strategies and ideas for working with families who are culturally and linguistically diverse. Although these strategies are meant to increase effectiveness when working with families from culturally diverse backgrounds, certainly these simple steps could also be applied to any and all families with which professionals work.

When adolescents enter adult life, their communication and relationship with their parents do not cease to exist. What professionals need to realize, and possibly remember from their own experiences, is that the communication and relationships between young adults and their families merely evolve. Rarely do parents' influences over lives simply end at the age of 18. Therefore, any adolescents' transition plan should document and reflect parental expectations and parental con-

Table 6.4
Possible Strategies for Working with Culturally Diverse Families

- Use endearing terms when speaking about the child.
- Avoid using stigmatizing labels.
- Avoid using vocabulary that parents could view as insulting.
- Try to "see" the child through the eyes of the parents.
- Be aware of nonverbal cues from the parents and to the parents from professionals.
- Be aware of language issues and provide interpreters when necessary.
- Be aware of any cultural beliefs/practices that could affect the student's transition plan.

tribution toward students' adult life (Ward et al., 2003). This is especially critical for culturally diverse families.

Ward and colleagues (2003) explored student and parent perspectives regarding their experiences with transition planning. They found that parents were more likely to report their experiences as being positive if they felt they were actively involved in the transition process. Having their opinions and suggestions valued by professionals helps them to feel empowered. Clearly, professionals who have drafts of plans, send copies of minutes, and invite them to every meeting command parental respect. Those who support and encourage parental participation and those who demonstrate dedication to students' best interests are held in high regard by parents. Overall, when professionals actively listen and seek advice, culturally diverse parents feel that they are a part of the decision making process. In addition, providing parents with resources can be beneficial to their participation. See Table 6.5 for possible web related resources for parents.

Table 6.5
Useful Web Resources for Collaborating with Families

Answers 4 Families

http://nncf.unl.edu/family/

This website offers a lot of information for families of children with special needs. There are articles and updates, special features, and links to other resources and services for families. There is also a list of links to other websites with important and current information on a variety of topics that could be of interest to parents.

Family Village

http://www.familyvillage.wisc.edu/education/inclusion.html

This page from the Family Village website, entitled "School & Community Inclusion," includes a list of links to organizations and websites that offer valuable information and resources for families of children with special needs and for special educators.

Continued on next page

Table 6.5 (continued)

LD Online

http://www.ldonline.org/ld_indepth/transition/transition.html

This page of the LD Online website deals with topics related to the transition planning process. There are resources that can be helpful to parents as well as teachers and other members of the IEP team. The page also contains links to articles and other websites that have information on specific topics within transition planning.

National Mental Health & Education Center

http://www.naspcenter.org/parents/parents.html

This website contains lists of links to resources for parents on topics such as school psychologists, ADD/ADHD, back to school issues, crisis resources, grade retention, success in school, No Child Left Behind, and more. There is also a list of handouts and NASP fact sheets that can be printed for reference.

Transition Planning Resource Guide For Families and Teens http://www.communityinclusion.org/transition/familyguide.html

This site contains a downloadable resource guide that families and students with disabilities can use to help them throughout the transition planning process. The complete guide can be downloaded, or the four sections of the guide can be downloaded separately. The resource guide does contain some information that is specific to Massachusetts, since it was created as a part of the Massachusetts Initiative for Youth with Disabilities; however, it also contains a good amount of information that is useful for parents in any state.

U.S. Department of Education

http://www.ed.gov/parents/needs/speced/resources.html

This page on the U.S. Department of Education website is titled "My Child's Special Needs" and contains links to information on a variety of topics related to disabilities, special education, and other education issues.

FINAL THOUGHTS

Getting a bit older and feeling independent for the first time can be a rush for many young people. For most adolescents and their families, thinking about postsecondary education, trade school, and/or employment after graduation can be experienced with feelings of joy and anxiety. The importance of transition planning for students with disabilities and their families should assist all stakeholders in the evolving responsibilities and relationships. However, only transition plans that represent a thoughtful unified vision will lead to a course of action that will result in optimal postsecondary school outcomes for students. In the end, professionals must learn to listen, appreciate, and respect values of students and families, including those from culturally and linguistically diverse backgrounds.

Chapter 7

JOB AND CAREER DEVELOPMENT: UNDERSTANDING THE NATURE AND TYPES OF JOBS

Darrah, an African-American female, is 15 years old and is currently a sophomore in high school. She has been diagnosed with a visual impairment and has limited vision in her left eye, with specific difficulties that include reading very small printed materials, tracking written material on the board, participating in some social situations, and making friends. In addition, she has a low level of self-confidence. Academically, her abilities are quite high and she does pretty well and falls in at about the middle to upper level in regards to her peers. She works well independently with the proper supports, but has more problems when required to work in a group setting. Clearly, she has some problems socially and does not use her needed supports since she does not want to draw any more attention to herself. Darrah's case manager, Mrs. Henry, is concerned about what she might do after graduation. It is time that Darrah started considering different types of jobs she would be interested in and what are different options she would need to get the skills to obtain those jobs. A positive note is that Darrah's parents communicate regularly with the teacher and regularly attend IEP meetings because they are very involved with helping their daughter. Mrs. Henry wants to clearly communicate to Darrah and her parents all the different options that are available to get the needed supports to be successful after graduation.

How might Mrs. Henry get Darrah and her parents to understand all of the options available to her after graduation? What could Mrs. Henry do to communicate clearly and effectively to Darrah and her parents? This chapter provides answers to these critical questions. Clearly, Darrah needs job and career development to discover the kinds of employment opportunities that are available to her. The employment picture in the early transition years for all youth is often characterized by holding several jobs for brief periods of time. Similarly, long-term employment is fairly rare among youth with disabilities out of school for up to two years. More than 60 percent of out-of-school youth with disabilities appear to have held their current or most recent job for six months or less. One-fourth of these children have held their job for six months to a year, 8 percent for one to two years, and only 5 percent for more than two years (NLTS, 2005). It is apparent that educators need to better prepare students to be more successful in the workforce.

The question then becomes, What do we know about different types of jobs for individuals with disabilities? Hotchkiss (2003) analyzed current populations survey data to investigate the status of workers with disabilities based on the definitions of the American with Disabilities Act (ADA, 1990). She found that workers with disabilities, taken as a group, were about six years older than other workers, worked about four fewer hours per week, and were more likely to be single and less likely to have a college degree. She also found that these workers continued to be disproportionately represented in low-growth, low-wage occupations. Compared to other workers, these workers were more likely to experience voluntary job separation and less likely to experience involuntary separation; and on average, they spent three weeks longer in the job search process. While it is common knowledge that the vast majority of persons entering real work settings, through either supported or competitive employment, enter jobs in the food services or learning areas, many of the jobs seem to be part-time in nature and seldom offer wages above the minimum wage or provide benefits, such as health-care coverage or paid vacations (Temelini & Fesko, 1996). Clearly, one must be aware of this trend and plan accordingly to better meet the needs of students so they can be successful participants in the community.

When considering possible job options for students, it is recommended that general and special educators follow some type of procedure or systematic approach. It is important that each student has the same opportunities at success and that each transition plan is individualized for each student. To keep consistency between students and within transition teams, a set of procedures is warranted. For example, a transition team may choose to use an ecological employment approach that matches individual interests with employer requirements and needs. As was mentioned in previous chapters it is very important that the student is a part of the transition process, along with his/her parents and family members, to choose a future job that he/she him/herself is interested in pursuing. If this facet of the process is accomplished, there will be a better match for both the individual and the employer. There is a growing awareness of the need to match individual interests and preferences to both job tasks and workplace cultures. Such an approach recognizes the importance of social and interpersonal relationships in the workplace (Kiernan & Schalock, 1997) and allows for a greater opportunity to identify critical networks and social support resources.

NEEDED JOB SKILLS AND VOCATIONAL ASSESSMENT

One of the most overwhelming obstacles that a student with a disability faces is assessing his/her own work skills. When many job seekers are asked by a job coach or trainer what work skills they have, many appear not to know. Job skills assessment should begin before skill and job questions have been asked. The job coach or trainer can determine much information regarding the client's work skills through observations and "mental notes" (Bennett, 2003). See Table 7.1 for a list of work skills that should be observed.

When it comes to skills that future employees need, many employers are willing to teach the hard skills (e.g., how to operate the machines) but appear unable to teach the other skills (e.g., initiative, punctuality, and efficiency). They sometimes do not have the time to teach these skills because of their many tasks. How do they train someone to care, to be conscientious, to be pleasant, or to have a positive attitude? Employers know they are much better off if they hire people with a good work ethic because they will be willing to learn what is needed to be successful on the job (Cheek, 2003). As a result, it is the job and responsibility of teachers and parents to help students develop positive skills through transition programming, training, and experiences.

Table 7.1
Needed Work Skills of Future Job Seekers

Work Skill	Examples
Dexterity	Assessing the ability to dial a telephone, package small items, file documents, attach postage and labels, write short telephone memos, assemble small components of a gadget, do craft-work, type, and use small machines.
Voice level, speech pattern, and confidence level in talking with others	Assessing the ability to answer the telephone or talk with a supervisor and subordinates and speak clearly, with appropriate volume, in a well-modulated tone, with a good work spacing pattern, ad confidence; and assessing the ability to talk with others who are familiar, new acquaintances, younger and older people, people of other races, gender, authority, and social standing.
Handling disagreement and unpleasant information	Assessing the ability to appropriately respond in stressful work situations, receive directions, work in a project group or decision-making group, and communicate with those in authority or subordinates.
Health and grooming condition	Assessing the ability of the individual to keep himself/herself groomed and clean as well as wearing clean clothes.
Effective communication	Observing the ability to understand directions, follow steps in a task, ask questions to clarify, communicate verbally, communicate with gestures and body language; and demonstrations of behavior and emotional expression, basic personality traits, and mental stability.

The assessment needed to assist professionals in planning for students to transition from school to all aspects of adult life include: (a) an analysis of background information (looking at existing records and documentation); (b) interviews or questionnaires (with the student, teachers, family members, and former employers); (c) psychometric instruments (standardized tests and interest inventories); (d) work samples (simulated job activities/tasks that can be used to assess an individual's interests, abilities, work habits, and personal and social skills); (e) curriculum-based assessment techniques (assessment based on what student has been taught in the curriculum and includes criterion-referenced testing, curriculum-based measurement, portfolio assessment, and performance-based assessment); and (f) situational assessment (the systematic observation process for evaluating behaviors in environments as close as possible to the individual's future living, working, or educational environment). More specifically, the situational assessment refers to the practice of conducting a 20- to 30-day evaluation of a student's performance in a structured vocational setting. In these assessment situations, the student is given an actual job to perform and information is collected on work skills and other work-related behaviors. Examples of work skills include the time required to learn new tasks, speed of performance, and accuracy, and examples of work-related behaviors are direction following, frustration tolerance, safety, motivation, punctuality, dependability, perseverance, and social-interpersonal skills (Biller, 1988).

To get the big picture of what a student can and cannot do and to help with transition planning, as many of the above assessments as possible should be incorporated into the assessment process. Because of the broad range and types of aptitudes and skills students possess, it is especially critical to evaluate each student as an individual who, like all other students, has different academic strengths, weaknesses, and learning styles. A current trend in career assessment incorporates the development of functional assessment systems to augment traditional assessment strategies. These methods are aimed at classifying and evaluating abilities needed to perform in the environment, and not at delineating diagnostic labels, traits, and aptitudes which characterize traditional approaches. Again, the assessment process should be consistently individualized for each student to get accurate results.

CHOOSING AN APPROPRIATE JOB

How do students choose a job that is appropriate for them? Clearly, some skills are needed to analyze job opportunities and skills and make good decisions on what jobs match needed skills. Students can be taught to gather information, arrange and rearrange this information looking for positive and negative characteristics, and then make the decision. Reflection and imagination are skills that should be used in examining all options. In other words, the better the information a person has when making a decision, the clearer the risks. Knowing the probability for each option allows the person to decide what risk is worth taking. The process of deciding is often cyclical in nature and students should be aware of this. A final decision does not have to be made if there is still information that is needed to help with the decision-making process. At the conclusion of the process, the person may decide to get more information and continue the process until a terminal decision is made. The process, therefore, recycles to the first step of stating a goal, with examination of new options, probabilities, and outcomes, and the eventual selection of a choice (Harrington, 1982).

Krumboltz and Baker (1973) described the decision making process of a job choice in a step-by-step sequence. According to them, individuals who accomplished decision-making skills did so by having developed the ability to learn about themselves and about career options, after considering a number of alternatives. These individuals had sought career-related information, clarified their values, made plans, had internal locus of control, engaged in exploratory activities with positive reactions, and overcame indecisiveness and its resultant anxiety. Apparently, students must learn about themselves in reference to the skills they are good at and those that they need to work on to improve. To use the above decision-making process, students must be taught this information and given opportunities in the classroom and other environments to practice the steps. To practicalize decision-making steps, general and special educators must help their students to:

- Solicit their goals and define the problem.
- Agree mutually to achieve the goals set forth.
- Generate alternative solutions to the problem.
- Collect information about alternatives to the situation.
- Examine the consequences of the options.
- Reevaluate the goals, alternatives, and consequences.
- Make the decision or tentatively select an alternative based on new developments and opportunities.
- Generalize the decision-making procedure to other problems.

COLLABORATION AND CONSULTATION
WITH RELATED PROFESSIONALS

Students with disabilities and their families tend to work with important professionals that include transition specialists, rehabilitation counselors, and/or job development specialists. These professionals provide different types of services. See Table 7.2 for some of the activities they could possibly provide (PACER Center, 1998).

Table 7.2
Possible Activities Provided by Transition-related Specialists

Transition-Related Specialist	*Possible Activities*
Transition Specialist	• Works with the student to identify preferences and goals. • Sets up opportunities for the student (or group of students) to learn about different careers through such activities as watching movies about careers, job shadowing, visiting different job environments, and hands-on activities that allow the student(s) to try out a job or aspects of a job. • Looks at what skills the student presently has and what skills he or she will need in the adult world. • Recommends coursework that the student should take throughout the remainder of high school to prepare for adult living (e.g., recreation, employment, postsecondary education, and independent living). • Identifies what job supports the student needs.
Rehabilitation Counselor	• Can be involved in a student's transition planning while he/she is still in school. • Typically works for the state's vocational rehabilitation (VR) agency, and helps people with disabilities prepare for and find employment.
Job Development Specialist	• Places the person on the job. • Trains the employee on job tasks and appropriate workplace behavior (this is usually done by a job coach who works intensively with the individual). • Talks with supervisor(s) and coworkers about disability awareness. • Provides long-term support to the employee on the job. • Helps to promote interaction between the employee and his or her coworkers.

Vocational preparation programs in the public schools must be responsive to an ever-changing job market. The content of these programs should reflect those occupations that are presently in demand and those that are projected to be available on the local, regional, and national levels. For students with disabilities, vocational mobility beyond the local community may be limited; consequently, vocational programs for these students need to be closely aligned with those specific occupations that are realistically available in the home community. Local job availability must be continually assessed by school personnel. Included in this career assessment activity are opportunities for students to participate in industrial tours, visits to community job sites, and exposure to the many activities and courses offered in the secondary school environment (Biller, 1988).

WORK-STUDY PROGRAMS

Another option for students with disabilities is a work-study program. Work-study employment involves part-time work for students, on or off the school campus that is sanctioned by the school. Through work-study, students learn basic as well as job-specific skills, and may receive school credit, pay, or both. This allows teachers, parents, and students to assess current, acquired, and needed skills that can be practiced and developed to be more employable in the future. The most common work-study placements are at food services (19%), maintenance jobs (16%), and clerical jobs (15%) (Cameto, Marder, Wagner, & Cardoso, 2003). According to this study, more than 90 percent of youth work-study jobs received school credit and/or pay for their work. Students typically received school credit (48%) or both pay and credit (28%), with 15 percent receiving pay only. This is another program option that should be considered for students. Typically, older youth are more likely than younger youth to have work-study jobs, but schools can work this type of arrangement into their transition process however they see fit. Again, individually planning and taking a student and family through the transition process using their wants, needs, and strengths will hopefully allow practitioners to choose the best transition option for the student.

TRADE AND TECHNICAL SCHOOLS

For proper transitioning to take place, students with disabilities must be provided with educational, vocational, and technical options. These options are tied to specific job-related careers and programs. Following are subsections that discuss these programs.

Vocational-Technical Education Programs

Vocational-technical education programs are often organized around specific occupational areas, including health occupation education, marketing and distributive education, home economics or consumer sciences education, trades and industrial education, business and office education, technical/communication, and agricultural education (Sarkees-Wircenski & Scott, 1995). In addition, out-of-school work experience programs are generally delivered under Cooperative Work Education (CWE). Students in CWE programs are supervised by a work experience teacher in an employment setting for half a day and spend the other time in school earning their academic credits. An obvious strength of this program is the opportunity to experience an actual job situation under the guidance of school personnel and an employer while earning academic credits at school at the same time.

Tech-Prep Programs

Tech-Prep programs generally require two years of secondary school in a vocational area followed by two years or more of higher education. These programs (e.g., drafting and nursing) often provide competency-based training and bridge the gap between secondary and postsecondary opportunities.

Career Academies

A career academy can be best described as "a school within a school," which focuses on a career theme (e.g., medical services and communications) and integrates technical and academic curricula. Career academies offer students a chance to concentrate in an occupational area while earning academic credits.

Youth Apprenticeships

Youth apprenticeships generally prepare students for skilled jobs in areas such as plumbing, carpentry, and other trade areas. Apprenticeship programs are usually operated by union or trade associations and students spend a certain number of hours in related employment settings while also taking courses that integrate academic and vocational instruction.

SUPPORTED AND COMPETITIVE EMPLOYMENT

Historically, efforts were placed on development of segregated training centers, specifically, sheltered workshops and craft centers. This was followed by recognition of the advantages to placement to training through the on-site supports of a job coach or employment training specialist, with the development of supported employment. Concerns about placement and inclusion in the workplace led to a more recent interest in the development of strategies that would access naturally occurring supports for persons with cognitive disabilities and other developmental disabilities at work (Kiernan, 2000). Supported employment evolved from research based on the belief that people with severe disabilities had the potential to secure and work productively in integrated community jobs. The concept of support employment was based on knowledge about how persons with disabilities learned, and how the economy was changing, and recognizing the benefits of a more inclusive work setting for persons with cognitive disabilities. Supported employment called for the placement of individuals into a real job by completing an analysis of job tasks and providing training for the individual in an actual workplace (Kiernan & Stark, 1986). Although the initial intent of supported employment was to assist individuals with more severe disabilities in entering employment, to date, most of the persons served through supported employment have been persons with less significant disabilities (Mank, 1994; Wehman & Kregel, 1995). Clearly, one of the characteristics of supported employment is that the person receives ongoing support services while on the job. This support is often provided by a job coach who helps the person learn to do the job and understand the rules, conventions, and expectations of the job site. The support continues to be provided as long as the person holds the job, although the amount of support may be reduced over time as the person becomes able to do the job more independently.

Competitive employment means a full-time or part-time job with competitive wages and responsibilities. Typically, competitive employment means that no long-term support is provided to the employee to help him or her learn the job or continue to perform the job. According to the Cameto et al. (2003), the most common regular jobs held by youth with disabilities are in maintenance (24%), personal care (19%), and food services (16%). The types of jobs youths hold change as they grow older, most noticeably between the ages of 15 and 16. Younger teens are most likely to hold jobs in maintenance and personal care, often in informal jobs such as gardening and baby-sitting. Older youth are more likely than younger teens to have food services, retail, and clerical jobs (Cameto et al., 2003).

JOB SEARCH METHODS AND INTERVIEWING

When considering employment for students, general and special education professionals must remember that job hunting is a long process which takes time and energy; and maintaining a positive disposition can be difficult. While job seekers with disabilities can become actively involved in the job search, they also need help maintaining the energy and optimism. Suggestions for professionals include having regular brief meetings with the individual to (a) discuss action steps and help maintain energy, (b) counsel the individual on what to expect during the search, (c) review the number of contacts and interviews it takes on average to secure a job, (d) develop a support plan for the job seeker, (e) determine areas in which the person will need support, and (f) plan supports accordingly. See Table 7.3 for a list of some job search axioms (Cheek, 2003).

Networking

General and special education must teach students that networking is one way to get a job. Networking refers to a process of interacting with the people one knows as well as with their contacts, communi-

Table 7.3
Job Search Axioms

- Everyone has problems getting a job, but most overcome them with creativity, resource-fulness, and effort.
- Some things are just beyond our control and we must move forward.
- Life is a journey and not a terminal activity. We must take each step as an opportunity to grow and not as a ending.
- You must live in the real world and be reasonable when setting goals and having expecta-tions.
- You cannot rewrite your past and you must accept where you are now and move forward.
- You must expect change and embrace it (every tomorrow offers the possibility of being better than today).
- No one can or will commit as much time to your job search as you can and should.
- The best opportunities are the ones you create.
- There is no magic bullet - just hard work.
- Perception can be reality and you can come across as a qualified and viable candidate for a job; you will be treated as such.

---

cating about one's interests and needs, and following up on their sug-gestions (Gandolfo & Graham, 1998). It is nothing more than a sys-tematic examination of the people one knows and deliberate outreach to them, based on the assumption that it is human nature to deal with people with whom one feels comfortable. Using personal connections as a key component of the job search can reduce the number of rejec-tions and decrease the amount of time a job search can take (see Gandolfo & Graham). A networking approach allows the job seeker to become an active participant in the process. After an individual identifies a job goal, the next step is to brainstorm any personal and professional connections the individual, family members, or profes-sionals have. These can be used to gain information, identify job leads, or introduce new contacts to the process. Many contacts will simply be used to help identify other people. A friend of a friend may be used to help identify other people and arrange an informational interview that provides face-to-face contact with others. These informational inter-views may lead to real job interviews and ultimate employment. Opening the door of a local business for a job seeker with disabilities for tours, or informational interviews increases the odds of his/her being considered for employment now or in the future (see Gandolfo & Graham).

Having a Resume

The goal of the resume is to get an interview. Everything on the resume should show the employer why the candidate should be hired. If a disability is evident, then the candidate can tackle any concerns by the employer regarding the disability in the interview. A mistake many writers make is to include information on a resume that is personal, or in a subtle way reveals difficulties or problems in designing an appropriate resume; students should use work experience that was performed in regular places of employment whenever possible. In addition, they should give references without being asked–these references can be friends and acquaintances (Bennett, 2003). Those involved with the transition process should be aware that the resume needs to be taught, practiced, and be a part of the curriculum for the student to be successful.

Having an Interview

In an interview, the job candidate has the opportunity to convince the employer that he/she is the best choice for the job. First, he/she must make sure that the resume has been delivered to the employer at least two days prior to the interview. It is absolutely necessary that the job candidate view the upcoming interview positively (Bennett, 2003). In the job interview, the candidate must talk about work duties he/she can do on the job (e.g., typing letters, trouble-shooting computers, transcribing medical records, doing accounts receivable, and managing staff). It is illegal for the employer to ask disability-related questions. The candidate with disabilities is wise not to bring up the subject of reasonable accommodation during the interview if the disability is not evident. At any time after obtaining the job, the individual can request reasonable accommodations (Bennett, 2003). It is important for the job interviewee to expect the employer to make some small talk to put him/her at ease. Some employers use the façade of a friendly conversation to get personal information that can not legally be asked in an interview. According to Bennett, the job seeker with disabilities, or his/her representative, must sense when the employer is leading the interview into areas which would disclose the candidate's disability and violate his/her rights under the Americans with Disabilities Act (ADA, 1990). To help students with disabilities, teachers and service providers must be thoughtful when planning instruction to make sure that students are given many opportunities to practice with corrective feedback to build competency over time.

TEACHING THE CRITICAL PROCESS

As professionals think about their roles in supporting job seekers with disabilities, it is crucial to remember that major transformations are occurring. First, the job seeker is moving from a passive to an active role. Next, once a job is found there will be logistical and physical issues to address. And finally, job seekers must mentally adjust to see themselves as workers rather than recipients of services (Gandolfo & Graham, 1998). General and special educators cannot assume that students with disabilities will just learn how to do all the things that have been discussed in this chapter. Students must be taught how to do all of these things to be successful. It is recommended that the following five components be implemented when teaching students with disabilities: daily review, presentation of material, guided practice, independent practice, and formative evaluation.

First, a daily review of previously instructed material ought to be delivered. Each class should begin with some type of review to measure if students remember and have retained information from the previous class. Second, the presentation of either new or old material must be carefully evaluated to reteach ideas or continue to the next level (Bakken, 1998). When presenting information, the instructor should model with examples and nonexamples making sure students have opportunities to discriminate. Third, guided practice must be instituted to allow the instructor and students to do examples together. Students should always get an opportunity to perform with teacher guidance before being asked to perform independently. Fourth, students should practice independently to demonstrate if they can perform the task on their own. This can also be referred to as homework. Finally, formative evaluation (consistent monitoring of daily tasks to check for understanding) should be instituted. It is important that professionals check students' work to see if they have grasped the concept they have instructed. If they have not, reteaching may be needed. Clearly, this is very likely since all the components discussed in this chapter are very complicated processes that will challenge students' proficiency.

FINAL THOUGHTS

The period that extends from the end of high school through a youth's twenties challenges youth with decisions regarding education, careers, marriage, and parenting in addition to other demands such as financial and residential independence. One of the clearest advantages of finishing high school is that it provides the necessary foundation for pursuing most opportunities beyond high school, which is critically important if youth with disabilities are to participate fully in any competitive economy. Career growth helps individuals to reach economic independence, personal growth and development, and expand his or her social support networks. To accomplish these essential steps, the student must be taught, guided, and given the appropriate opportunities to be successful. As a result, we must help through coaching, training, support, and advice. While treating them like any other job seeker, we must also counsel them on the most appropriate attitudes and successful actions and responses to ensure that they obtain and keep the jobs they want and deserve.

Chapter 8

EMPLOYMENT TRAINING, SUPPORT, AND VOCATIONAL/TECHNICAL EDUCATION

Elijah, an African-American male, is 17 years old and is currently a junior in high school. He has an educational diagnosis of a developmental disability, with an intelligence quotient (IQ) of 55 and has difficulties in reading, mathematics, written expression, social skills, organizational skills, and adaptive behaviors. He reads just above the first grade level but is a good listener and wants to get better at reading. In math, he is in a functional curriculum working on money skills, measurement (for cooking), and reading a clock. Elijah can write his name and phone number but is still working on his address and other personal information. He does a very nice job following directions, but when he is not in a one-on-one situation, he tends to get off task. His parents are very supportive and communicate regularly with his teachers and case manager as they work on his skills at home as well as in school. In both environments (home and school), Elijah is working on being more independent and focused as well as making good choices and decisions. After high school, his parents would like him to be as independent as he possibly can. They would like him to hold a job, but they know he will probably need some type of support system and training to do this. Clearly, they would like him to be able to live with others so that he may have more social opportunities. Elijah is interested in living away from his parents and holding a job. Currently, he is interested in working with wood and metals as well as with repairing things that are broken (i.e., a toaster or a lawn mower)–these might be two areas to investigate for possible future career choices.

For each student, an individual transition plan needs to be developed considering the viewpoints of the student, parents, and family members to help develop individual career aspirations. General and special education teachers and professionals need to be apprised of all the different options and opportunities for students with disabilities after high school. By considering the skills and needs of students and knowing all the possible options for them, teachers and professionals can work together to develop the best possible transition programs. Based on Elijah's case, the questions are: What types of employment opportunities are available and what skills are needed to be successful to help him after high school? How will the needed skills will be trained, where will they will be trained, and what kind of ongoing support will be provided for him? This chapter responds to these critical questions.

When planning for the transition of students with disabilities, there tends to be two types of programming available in the schools: career education and vocational programs. Career education programs provide a general background in preparation for employment and adulthood and in helping students to make appropriate choices. Vocational education programs provide specific skill and competency preparation sequences that are needed for students after they have selected a particular career path and vocation (Luft, Koch, Headman, & O'Connor, 2001). Training of needed skills and competencies is important for students with disabilities so that they can transition from high school to the workforce and community. Career and vocational education represent two of the most important training avenues through which students with disabilities acquire transition preparation. If either programming or planning in these areas is poorly implemented, students are unlikely to acquire the knowledge, skills, and work competency levels to obtain and keep a job in the community (Luft et al., 2001).

EMPLOYMENT OPPORTUNITIES

Getting a job can be a very difficult process for anyone; add a disability and it could be even more difficult. Two basic facts that critically emerge about employment of people with disabilities are that there is a high rate of unemployment and that they are more likely to rely on agencies to get jobs. Getting a job is hard work. On average, it takes 10 to 20 calls to arrange an interview and 7 to 10 interviews to secure a job (Gandolfo & Graham, 1988). General and special educators must develop job skills needed by students with disabilities to prepare for the workforce and independently secure a job for themselves.

Job Development

The task of job development is one of generating a pool of job placement alternatives so that there are real choices to be made when looking for the best possible placement. One of the most commonly suggested activities is a community survey. A community survey identifies the local job areas that (a) have vacancies, (b) anticipate vacancies frequently because of high turnover rates, and (c) hire nonskilled, entry-level employees (Clark & Kolstoe, 1995). Another procedure in job development is to identify areas for job creation within the community's labor market. This is a task requiring some skill in analyzing jobs and some creativity in using the analyzed data for proposing new jobs. This can occur through the creation of a new job by combining elements of existing jobs or by creating entirely new jobs to fulfill unmet needs of the employer (see Clark & Kolstoe).

Job Analysis

A necessary element of job development is a job analysis. A job analysis is a systematic way of determining the specific demands of any job. Typically, the purpose is to assess a specific work environment for a specific job. However, it can help plan for the instruction of needed skills. Job requirements, characteristics of the work setting, and an indication of every anticipated demand give the placement specialist highly useful information for every placement (Clark & Kolstoe, 1995).

Work-Site Modifications

Another important facet of deciding on possible jobs entails the school personnel to evaluate jobs as to whether a work-site modification is needed for the student. Work-site modifications can be defined as work-related changes that enable a person with a disability to be employed (Hester & Stone, 1984). They range from the simplest and least costly ones (changing work procedures, change task assignments, changing work locations, or changing hours) to the most expensive, most complex ones like using technology or rehabilitation engineering for sophisticated equipment or building adaptations. School-based job developers and job trainers need to use work-site modifications not only to provide better access to employment under the employment provisions of ADA but also to increase the creative aspects of possible job alternatives (Clark & Kolstoe, 1995).

TRAINING FOR NEEDED SKILLS

When considering different employment opportunities, general and special educators must consider skills needed by students with disabilities to be successful. Young people with disabilities often do not possess the skills and qualifications necessary to compete for jobs. Many are unable to access further education and training largely because of the lack of specialized facilities, learning materials, and on-site personal care and support (Elrod, 1987; Taylor, McGilloway, & Donnelly, 2004). For example, Elrod identified academic skills that are prerequisite to success in vocational courses. The most frequent skills are basic math skills (measurement and computation using fractions, decimals, and mixed numbers) and the ability to read at seventh- to tenth-grade levels. Having good social skills is also needed to be successful at work. Social skills have been recognized as a necessary factor in job getting and maintenance (Hall, Ford, Moss, & Dineen, 1986). Educators and professionals must provide opportunities for students to develop academic and social skills. Brolin (1989, 1996) recognized the importance of social skills and suggested the use of the he Life-Centered Career Education Model (LCCE) that integrates career education into the regular education curriculum using a three-dimensional model addressing 22 basic life-centered competencies. The comprehensive nature of this program, its integration of regular and special education programs, and its extensive support materials make this a viable choice for the transition team. See Table 8.1 for a list of the competencies (Brolin, 1996).

Table 8.1
Competencies Preparing Students for Future Life Roles

Daily Living Skills

1. Managing personal finances
2. Selecting and managing a household
3. Caring for personal needs
4. Raising children and meeting marriage responsibilities

Continued on next page

Table 8.1 (continued)
5. Buying, preparing, and consuming food
6. Buying and caring for clothing
7. Exhibiting responsible citizenship
8. Utilizing recreational facilities and engaging in leisure
9. Getting around the community

Personal-Social Skills

10. Achieving self-awareness
11. Acquiring self-confidence
12. Achieving socially responsible community behavior
13. Maintaining good interpersonal skills
14. Achieving independence
15. Making adequate decisions
16. Communicating with others

Occupational Guidance and Preparation

17. Knowing and exploring occupational possibilities
18. Selecting and planning occupational choices
19. Exhibiting appropriate work habits and behaviors
20. Seeking, securing, and maintaining employment
21. Exhibiting sufficient physical-manual skills
22. Obtaining specific occupational skills

Models for Teaching Skills

When considering the needed skills for students with disabilities, skill instruction should occur in the classroom, at home, and in the community. In other words, skill instruction should include peers at school and adults and peers in the community. To provide skill training, schools may decide to adopt a training model discussed below.

• *The School-Based Career Development and Transition Education Model* (Clark & Kolstoe, 1995). This is an excellent model for planning services that offer options across a range of disabilities, beginning at prekindergarten levels with the acquisition of basic job and living skills. This program is unique for specifying a range of possible secondary school options, including cooperative education, work evaluation, and technical education. In addition, it identifies specific employment outcomes at various stages of the development process: entry-level jobs, semiskilled or specialized jobs, specialized or technical jobs, and professional or managerial jobs (Luft et al., 2001).

- *The Experience-Based Career Education Modell* (EBCE, 1976; Larson, 1981). This was developed using a cooperative education model. EBCE can be used particularly as an exploratory experience to teach about work with students working as volunteers without pay. Work sites are changed according to student needs and interests to give them exposure to work environments and experience a variety of work cultures. This might help students to decide what type of job they might want to pursue after high school.

- *The Mentoring Model* (Farren, Gray, & Kaye, 1984). This model identifies business mentors to act as sponsors, teachers, coaches, and other role models as needed by the student and his/her environment. It provides the student with fairly specific learning experiences related to an identified occupation through advice and coaching of a mentor (Anderson & Strathe, 1987). Clearly, contact within the community would be necessary for this program to be successful as well as contact with the mentor on the success of the student.

- *Supported Employment Model* (Clark & Kolstoe, 1995; Moon, Goodall, Barcus, & Brooke, 1986). In this model the trainer is responsible for teaching all job skills, for training non-work skills that are related to the job (e.g., social expectations, transportation, and grooming), and for advocacy of the student. The phases of direct instruction in job and job-related are job orientation and assessment, initial training and skill acquisition, and skill generation and maintenance/fading (Moon et al., 1986). See Table 8.2 for a description of each (Clark & Kolstoe, 1995).

Table 8.2
Job-Related Skills

Job-Related Skills	Description
Job Orientation and Assessment	This phase of job training may last from a couple weeks to a month. The trainer has to keep in mind that the employer expects the work to be performed up to standards while the training takes place. This means that the trainer must start with learning all the tasks related to the job and do a great deal of modeling for job and job-related skills. The technique of demonstration, followed by student performance and immediate reinforcement, is critical.

Continued on next page

Table 8.2 (continued)

Job-Related Skills	Description
Initial Training and Skill Acquisition	Performance data must be recorded by the trainer during training and skill acquisition. The two types of data that are critical are those that indicate (a) how the trainee per forms a job duty without promoting a nonnaturally occurring reinforcement, and (b) the number and kinds of prompts (verbal, physical, or modeling) that the trainee needs to perform the job duty. The focus during this phase is for the trainee to acquire accuracy and independence. Training for job-related skills such as appropriate dress, using a pay telephone, punching in and out on a time-clock, coffee break behavior, using a vending machine, or riding a city bus should also occur during this initial phase. The job coach and trainee have to arrange time before or after work hours or during lunch or coffee breaks to work on these skills since only work skills should be worked on during work time.
Fading	The fading phase involves the gradual removal or fading out of the job trainer. This process could take a few days to a week for high-functioning trainees to months for low-functioning trainees. The job trainer must slowly and systematically withdraw from the job and the trainee. The final goal at the outset must be worker independence to enhance productivity that meets the company's standards.

With regard to fading, the actual schedule of fading is determined not only by the trainee's job performance but also by the needs and personalities of the supervisor and coworkers and the characteristics of the job and the job site. It is possible that some trainees will need some support indefinitely to maintain their independent productivity. This support will have to be provided by a supervisor or coworkers. The job coach training specialist will have to train these individuals before terminating the job-site training, and be alert to changes in personnel so that reentry into the job site for training of new personnel can occur. Developing natural support systems in a work site is critical and requires some careful planning and implementation (Mangan, 1992; Nisbet & Hagner, 1988).

ON-SITE TRAINING

Students with disabilities need work experiences in the community that progress from part-time to full-time employment after graduation (Luft et al., 2001). This may require on-site, on-the-job training that should continue until the worker begins to perform all functions to the satisfaction of the employer (Hall et al., 1986). Regarding possible training approaches, Danley and Anthony (1987) provided some possible approaches that have been used by placement personnel with people with disabilities. See Table 8.3 for a description of approaches.

Table 8.3
Possible Job Training Approaches

Training Approach	*Description*
Train-Place	Train-place is the traditional model in which the placement specialist places a person with disabilities in a job for which he/she has been trained. The area of training is presumably determined through some type of assessment. Training may be provided at school (e.g., laundry and horticulture), in a training program separate from school (e.g., cosmetology), or in the community.
Place-Train	Place-Train is a model that has come out of the supported employment movement. Placement occurs directly in the community and training occurs on the job site where continued employment is expected.
Choose-Get-Keep	Choose-Get-Keep begins with the basic assumption that persons with disabilities, and especially those with psychiatric disabilities, need to choose not only what kind of work they will do but also the type of work and specific location to establish the best person-job match. It also provides for the individual to secure the job himself or herself so that there are clear choices for both the individual and the employer. This approach follows the supported employment model with time-limited or ongoing support for the person to assure that he or she will keep the job as long as it is desirable.

Continued on next page

Table 8.3 (continued)

Training Approach	Description
Train-Place-Train	In Train-Place-Train a student is first given some basic occupational and prevocational training at school in a regular vocational education, adapted vocational education, or special occupational training program in the community through a work experience training program. Placement is then arranged in a job site in the community and specific training is provided to ensure that all aspects of the employment situation have been addressed.

As professionals think about their roles in supporting job seekers with disabilities, it is crucial to remember that major transformations are occurring. First, the job seeker is moving from a passive to an active role where he/she is in charge of his/her own actions. Next, once a job is found there will be logistical and physical issues to address to make sure student needs and job requirements match. And finally, job seekers must mentally adjust to see themselves as workers rather than recipients of services. As they become more independent, they should be informed about available supports (Gandolfo & Graham, 1988).

It is common knowledge that there are differences in basic physical and intellectual performance levels. An intelligent, highly motivated, student who has a hearing impairment may require half the job training time that a student who is moderately learning disabled might require for the same job. Job trainers must look at speed of learning all job tasks from an individual basis and plan for job training time based on each student's performance. Furthermore, they must analyze performance errors to determine the kind of training the student specifically needs (Clark & Kolstoe, 1995).

General and special educators must understand that some career skills cannot be taught effectively in school-based programming (e.g., mobility in the community; using stores and laundromats; and developing hobbies, recreational, and social interaction skills). Because students with disabilities have difficulty generalizing from one setting to another, classroom-based instruction is often not sufficient (Luft et al., 2001). Community-based instruction offers the individual the potential for social and personal fulfillment and participation in productive and work-related activities. Sometimes, however, it is not possible for students to leave school grounds. When this occurs, sites and tasks can be identified within the school or on the grounds that can approximate natural community environments (Wehman, 1996). The goal must be to prepare students in the classroom and in work experiences in the school knowing that educators are supplementing or preparing students for off-site experiences. On the other hand, although not something that is discussed, there is always that possibility that there will be job failure. Many times job failure is a result of individuals not receiving appropriate feedback on how they are doing or performing. Other factors include a lack of needed education and training and poor management by parents, guardians, and social service agencies. Improved support and training by social workers could help with each of these problems (Hall et al., 1986).

THE NEED FOR CONTINUING SUPPORT

Once students proceed through academic and job specific training and obtain a job, it is important for school transition staff to maintain and continue support of the student with a disability. Unless a worker is able to advocate strongly on his or her own behalf, has good family support, or has skilled professional input, all forms of advocacy may be lost. Without a place to turn for help in solving problems, opportunities for job failure are almost infinite (Hall et al., 1986). School transition staff could do different things to support a student with a disability in a work environment. They could mail the supervisor evaluations on schedule and respond immediately if any problems are indicated. In addition, they could visit the job site and monitor the worker's performance by talking to supervisors and coworkers and by completing task analytic probes, production rate recordings, and nontask observations. Clearly, the transition staff should keep up with management and supervisor changes at the job site as personnel changes can seriously affect job performance. Also important is keeping in touch with the family so they can find out about any changes in the worker's home situation. Lastly, the transition staff should be prepared to go back on the job site at any time for retraining skills needed by the individual to be successful in performing the desired job (Moon et al., 1986).

Once the worker is able to perform all functions of the job to the employer's satisfaction and the placement staff has withdrawn, follow-up or employment support service begins. This service includes a wide variety of activities designed to keep the worker with disabilities employed and typically includes additional training in specific vocational or nonvocational areas, counseling with the employer or other staff members, reevaluation of both skills and speed of performance, modification of job requirements, and occasionally removal of the trainee for additional training or placement at another job. If a trainee is fired for poor performance, retraining is required. However, monitoring takes the form of visits for as long as the person is based on employee performance (Hall et al., 1986). Regardless of the kind of job or the nature of the work setting, there are some basic information questions that a job supervisor must ask (and even probe for) to find out how students are performing. According to Clark and Kolstoe (1995), these possible questions are:

- Is the student performing up to company standards? If not, why?
- Is the student improving, performing consistently, or doing less well than during the last visit?
- Are there any job-related skill problems? If so, what are they?
- Have there been any changes in the job duties or job-related expectations? If so, what are they?
- Is there anything that the student needs or wants from the school in the way of additional support or assistance?
- Is the "honeymoon" over for one or more of the participants? For Whom? What led to that determination?

The role of job supervisor involves monitoring and evaluating the progress of student workers in a job placement. Specifically, it involves the monitoring and evaluation of the job placement itself, which includes observation of every aspect of the job analysis to determine any changes that work against a job match. Following are four types of supervisory visits that could be made over the duration of the school's involvement in the work-training program (Clark & Kolstoe, 1995):

- Regularly scheduled visits to follow up on the student's performance and the work setting itself. They are routinely expected by the student, the student's parents, and the employer.

- Scheduled visits to address problems or concerns that are beginning to have negative effects on the student's performance or that are expected to have some effect in the near future. They may result from observations made in previous supervisory visits; comments from the employer, job supervisor, or coworkers; reports from teachers or staff at school; or concerns expressed by parents.

- Unscheduled visits to deal with a crisis. They arise out of emergency situations in which a responsible school representative is needed to deal with a crisis.

- Scheduled or unscheduled visits after a student is no longer in formal training and is employed. They are important to show continued support for the former student and the employer, and they create follow-up opportunities to get longitudinal feedback on the program.

VOCATIONAL EDUCATION

Vocational education and experiences are very important and beneficial for students with very positive outcomes. For instance, students with disabilities who take vocational courses or participate in work experience programs tend to have fewer absences, succeed more in their courses, and graduate more often from high school (Evers, 1996). Students having vocational classes and work experiences in high school also were the best predictors of those who earned the highest wages (Shapiro & Lentz, 1991). Lastly, two factors associated with a dramatically lower probability of dropping out of high school in the eleventh and twelfth grades are a concentration in vocational courses or having taken a survey vocational education class (U.S. Department of Education, 1994).

Vocational education provides skill and knowledge preparation for employment where career education prepares the student for a lifetime of work and adult roles (Luft et al., 2001). Vocational education is that critical portion of job-related academic work skills that moves a student who has made a career choice and makes him/her "job ready." It forms a critical preparation stage that occurs just prior to a student beginning his/her work career. Typically, vocational education programs provide "(a) preparation for jobs requiring less than a baccalaureate degree; (b) activities and experiences whereby one learns to assume a primary work role; (c) an emphasis on skill development or specific job preparation; (d) a focus of attention at the upper-middle grades, senior high, and two-year postsecondary levels; and (e) a program, rather than an educational philosophy, with the major goal being gainful employment"(Meers, 1987, p. 22). Of primary importance is the requirement that vocational programs deliver academic and job-related information to students in curricula that are clearly related to the workplace and that students realize are beneficial to their program (Green & Weaver, 1994). While it is important to begin the development of nonacademic skills early, experiences at the secondary level should not be ignored. Vocational and prevocational training programs are important–their curricula must ensure that positive work attitudes, habits, and personal-social skills, such as problem solving and getting along with others, become a part of the student's repertoire of skills upon completing training (DeMario, 1992). Clearly, the goal of these programs is to shape and form a student who can become a productive citizen in society.

CAREER AND TECHNICAL EDUCATION

Another option for students is career and technical education. Career and technical education (CTE) can benefit students directly by providing earning advantages both before and after graduation. It can provide indirect benefits by increasing student engagement, retention, and persistence and by directing them to postsecondary education and the pursuit of lifelong learning. Career and technical education programs motivate students to get involved in their learning by engaging them in problem-solving activities that lead to the construction of knowledge and by providing them with hands-on activities that enable them to apply that knowledge. In addition, CTE programs bring students and adults (parents, teachers, and community leaders) together in a setting of collaborative learning. They offer opportunities for students to interact with community members potential employers, and students and teachers who share similar career/vocational interests through organizations such as Future Farmers of America (Ball, Garton, & Dyer, 2001). Career and technical education programs offer students an alternative to college preparatory programs that they may not have the interest, ability, or skills to pursue and prepare them for the future at the same time (Cohen & Besharov, 2002). Researchers (see Cardon, 2000; Harvey, 2001) have shown that students who are considered to be "at risk" or "disadvantaged" as well as students with disabilities have greater success after high school when they are enrolled in technology education, technology preparatory (tech prep), school-to-career, and other CTE programs.

As it stands, regional vocational-technical schools (RVTS) are often more competitive than the public secondary school. Whereas the public secondary school is likely to place a great deal of stress on training for positions requiring minimal skills (e.g., electronic assembly), the vocational-technical school seeks to train for higher level positions (e.g., electronic diagnostician). The RVTS generally operates on a regional basis and draws applicants from a number of school districts, except in large cities. By virtue of experience in a trade area and familiarity with the standards of employers, the trade area instructor has a fairly good idea of what an employer expects as entry level competence. In this regard, the special education teachers perform a supporting role via a resource center or by direct participation in the classroom. It is not uncommon to find the special education teacher directly involved in the activities of the trade area. He/she may be assisting the instructor to modify instruction or may be assisting the youngster to comprehend a task. Generally, he/she provides continuity in the individual program of the student and meets with the child on a regular basis for approximately one period per day, five days per week. In the ninth grade, most youngsters spend one-half of their time in academic programs and one-half of their time exploring various trades (e.g., they may spend a few days each in as many as 10 different trade areas). This provides the student with an opportunity to become acquainted with a variety of trade options, and it provides the instructor with an opportunity to screen the individual. Once a trade area decision is made, the student will ordinarily spend the remaining three years in a program focusing on that trade (Cawley, Kahn, & Tedesco, 1989).

CONSIDERING CHOICES FOR STUDENTS

If there is a transition process incorporated in a school building or system, general and special education professionals will be better prepared to help with the transition of their students. As indicated in the earlier parts of this book, four components of this process are career awareness, career exploration, career preparation, and career assimilation. Career awareness is emphasized with elementary school experiences with basic home and health care, developing a sense of self-worth and confidence, and developing positive attitudes about work. Career exploration begins in elementary school but has a real focus in middle school. Students begin to investigate their own unique abilities, needs, and interests in terms of work, leisure, recreation, and other potential life roles. Career preparation is the focus of the high school years, especially for those not considering some type of postsecondary training. During these years, the team needs to focus on the 22 competencies previously mentioned. Lastly, career assimilation occurs during high school and incorporates work experiences in the students preferred career, beginning with part-time and moving towards full-time employment (Luft et al., 2001).

When considering a job for a student, it is important to include all aspects of the world of work that are important to the student's future success. This includes information about occupational roles, occupational vocabulary, occupational alternatives, and information related to realities to the world of work. General and special education professionals must understand that their students may not have as many experiences working as other students. This lack of work-related exposure results in adolescents who may face transition planning with little or no incidental background knowledge of what work entails and what their potential work interests may be (Luft et al., 2001). The lack of incidental learning experiences can be a concern as the foundations for values about work, the desire to work, and work ethics support job acquisition and maintenance are formed in these early experiences (Symanski & Hershenson, 1998). Thus, educational and transition professionals must provide divergent work experiences as early as possible to learn about students' qualities and work habits as well as for them to learn about themselves.

When considering specific jobs for students with disabilities a systematic approach should be implemented. A systematic approach to job placement uses well-established procedures, job analysis, an analysis of individual assessment, job work-site modification, and job matching (Clark & Kolstoe, 1995). Educational and transition professionals must consider if a job is appropriate for students or not. They may decide against a job because there is inconsistent supervision, nonexistent supervision, frequent changes in supervision, inappropriate environment, bad working hours, inappropriate location, poor pace of work activity, dangers or hazards, or incompatibility of the work situation with a student's interests (Parrish & Kok, 1985). It is their job to adapt or modify the choice a student has made as needed. Students with disabilities may make a selection of a career, begin skill training, and determine that this initial choice is no longer appropriate. In such cases, the team of professionals must provide additional experiences to help the student make a more satisfying choice or move the student between introductory career and vocational experiences for some time before making a final selection (Luft et al., 2001). This can be an ongoing process that could take some time—each individual case must be treated appropriately.

FINAL THOUGHTS

There are many employment opportunities for students with disabilities. Our students, however, need the proper training of skills, on-site training of specific jobs, and continuous support from teachers, parents, transition coordinators, and employers to be successful. Since students with disabilities often do not generalize from one situation or setting to another, we need to do more than just classroom-based instruction and train students in the "real world" so that this process has more of a meaning and impact knowing that some students will need more training and support than others. As students progress through high school years, general and special education professionals must be aware that they need instruction with increasing amounts of responsibility in job roles. As they get older, the complexities of the "real world" also need to be addressed by adding daily living responsibilities to their job roles as well. As professionals, we must remember to work closely with students and parents to make sure our transition plan is in line with what they want so that the work experience they get will be motivating to them as well as seen as a type of training that proves beneficial in future employment. Choosing an appropriate job, work setting, program delivery, and type of support should all be individualized for each student with a disability. Every decision should consider the wants and needs of the individual as well as their parents along with the skills they have and those they need to learn. In addition, the amount of support and accommodations should be discussed with all those involved (e.g., students, parents, and employers). All students with disabilities need to have the opportunity for successful employment; and if there is a plan in place with appropriate procedures, this can happen.

Chapter 9

SOCIAL OUTCOMES AND COMMUNITY RESOURCES

Ricardo, a Hispanic American male, is 16 years old and is currently a sophomore in high school. He has been diagnosed as having emotional or behavioral disorders, with specific social skill problems in school and community settings. Academically, Ricardo has all the abilities to do well in all of his subjects, but his lack of appropriate social skills tends to affect his performance. He can work independently pretty well but has significant problems when required to work in a group setting or with other students. When working with others, he has difficulty taking turns, listening to others, and receiving feedback to name just a few. Ricardo's case manager, Mrs. Tavarez, is concerned about Ricardo getting the necessary social skills training needed to be successful in school and after graduation. Additionally, Ricardo's parents are concerned about his social skills as they see the same problems occurring at home as in school. Clearly, he cannot hold a job because of his lack of social skills.

How might Mrs. Tavarez get Ricardo's parents to work with her to help with his social skill deficits? What could Mrs. Tavarez do to incorporate social skills training into her transitional curriculum? How will social skills be taught so that Ricardo will learn appropriate ways to work with and deal with others? Surely, the current transition program needs to be changed or modified so that he may obtain needed skills to function appropriately in and out of school. This is the focus of this chapter.

Transition programs for young adults with disabilities frequently focus on preparation for employment. In fact, the focus on these programs is to prepare students for life after high school, which is often the world of work. Beirne-Smith, Ittenbach, and Patton (1998) noted that some of these students can learn vocational skills. However, many of these students may not be successful in finding appropriate jobs and staying employed long after graduation (Wehman, 1992). Failure to maintain successful employment often relates to difficulty in developing social interpersonal skills (Goldstein & Morgan, 2002; Wolfe, Boone, & Blanchett, 1998); and thus, some students need more direct instruction and opportunities to practice social skills in developmentally appropriate vocational and educational settings (Goldstein & Morgan, 2002; Wehman, 1992; Wehmeyer, 1992). As it appears, many students are currently not getting the social skills instruction needed to be successful after high school. In order to meet the social skills needs of students with disabilities, it is important for general and special education teachers to create a classroom environment where all students can learn and practice these skills. They must realize that students need to exhibit proper social skills in common tasks suitable for group work, small-group learning, interdependence, individual accountability and responsibility, and cooperative behavior (Davidson, 1994). In addition, they must realize that the lack of social skills lead to aggression, rejection by peers, academic failure, loneliness, social dissatisfaction, difficulty maintaining employment and relationships, and contact with the legal system (Parker & Asher, 1997).

DEVELOPMENT OF SOCIAL SKILLS

As public school populations grow in diversity, school personnel are increasingly challenged to understand and meet different behaviors students bring to the classroom. School personnel must be able to differentiate between cultural differences and behavioral deficits; and they must use culturally relevant and effective practices to bring about behavior change and be committed to the growth of every child no matter how great the difference or severe the behavior (Cartledge & Milburn, 1996). Since schools are under pressure to create safe, orderly, and effective learning environments where students acquire social as well as academic skills that will allow them to succeed in school and beyond, they must support the development of a school-wide culture of competence that incorporates social skills instruction that is an integral part of the school's curriculum and daily operations (Sugai & Lewis, 2004). Social skills need to be taught as students with disabilities will not just "pick up" appropriate skills that are needed to be successful in school, the community, and the workforce. During any given school day, students encounter a variety of settings, for example, the school bus, hallway, classroom, cafeteria, playground, and gym. Each setting requires specific social skills for successful interactions with others sharing in the same space and these skills need to be instructed for students to acquire and use them appropriately.

Importance of Social Skills

Social skills are important to function effectively in school, the community, and the workforce (Strain & Odom, 1986). Social skills form the basis for social competence. Gresham, Sugai, and Horner (2001) stated that the dimensions of social skills are peer relational skills, self-management skills, academic skills, compliance skills, and assertion skills; and they defined social competence as "the degree to which students are able to establish and maintain friendships, and terminate negative or pernicious interpersonal relationships" (p. 331). In addition, the development of social relationships may contribute to the self-determination and community integration of students with disabilities (Berry & Hardman, 1998; Schleien, Tipton, & Green, 1997).

Many students with disabilities lack adequate social interaction skills, are at risk later in life in terms of social adjustment or life functioning, and need direct instruction concerning social interaction skills to overcome deficits. Social skill deficits put students with disabilities at risk because of the interrelationships among social competence with other, long-term life functions (Stumbo, 1995). In addition, interaction skills are highly related to overall life adjustment and later functioning in the community (Gresham, Elliott, & Black, 1987). Clearly, effective social problem solving requires reading one's own and others' feelings, and being able to accurately label and express those feelings. Such skills are aspects of social and emotional learning (Zins, Elias, Weissberg, Greenberg, Haynes, & Frey, 1998). Well-developed social skills can help youth with disabilities develop strong and positive peer relationships, succeed in school, and begin to successfully explore adult roles such as employee, coworker/colleague, and community member. Social skills also support the positive development of healthy adult relationships with family members and peers. Improving students' social skills and social acceptance involves cooperative group learning (e.g., Johnson & Johnson, 1994; Quinn, Jannasch-Pennell, & Rutherford, 1995). Cooperative learning is where students work in groups of three to four students as a team towards a common learning goal. Earlier, Kagan (1992) differentiated among three different approaches to social skills development through cooperative learning, namely: the natural, the formal, and the structured natural approaches. When educators apply the natural approach, no instruction in social skills is provided with the belief that skills will be acquired naturally as students engage in cooperative learning activities. At the opposite end of the spectrum, educators who practice the formal approach emphasize direct social skill instruction as a defining component of the cooperative learning lesson. General and special education teachers applying the structured natural approach adopt a social skill of the week. The instructional component for the structured natural approach includes the teacher introducing the skill, discussing and demonstrating student-generated answers to nonverbal and verbal demonstrations of the skill, modeling and reinforcing the skill, and reflecting on the skill. In order to be effective, transition programs must incorporate the development of social skills in a natural setting, where students with and without disabilities will benefit from interactions (Wehman, 1992) and where social skills may be practiced in different environments (e.g., school, home, and work).

TEACHING APPROPRIATE SOCIAL SKILLS

To prepare students with disabilities to be successful after high school, it is necessary to teach them the appropriate social skills. Adequate social skills need to be acquired while students are still enrolled in school and further supported and refined in postsecondary, community, and work settings (Bremer & Smith, 2004). Therefore, helping students learn social skills in a positive and supportive environment will help to minimize the impact of different disabilities on school success. In community life, appropriate social behaviors may be even more important than academic or job skills in determining whether one is perceived as a competent individual (Black & Langone,

1997). Nonetheless, students must see the need for the skills being taught. In a school setting, general and special education teachers may ask students to identify social skills necessary for achieving goals important to them. Based on such discussions, students and educational professionals can jointly select one or two skills to work on at a time (Bremer & Smith, 2004). These professionals must be aware what skills students need to be successful and may just need to decide what skills are instructed based on there own expertise and observations.

Social skills will probably need to be taught to students with disabilities for them to acquire needed skills to be successful. Social skill instruction may begin early in preschool and primary grades, when the child is most receptive to behavior change. Good social skill instruction early in the child's life can be instrumental in minimizing or preventing problem behaviors, which are likely to become more severe or resistant in later years (Cartledge, 2005). Social skills instruction, however, can be taught at any level with any type of student that needs essential skills to be successful. Adolescence is also a critical time in the social world in terms of self-evaluation and self-confidence. Healthy social interaction is important and helps to prepare youth for normal adult functioning, including independence and fitting into a work environment (Bauminger, 1990). Individual lessons can be developed to meet the needs of *all* students who need social skills instruction. The lessons, however, must be tailored to the learners so that instructional activities might be revised and intensified accordingly. Instructional pace and movement through the curriculum must be based on skill acquisition, not simply focused on covering the material. Further, lessons must reflect genuine need. Students are more likely to be responsive, and growth more evident, if they see a real purpose in the social skill instruction they receive. Additionally, instruction needs to differentiate between those who possess the skill in their behavioral repertoire, but will not perform it, and those who do not know how to perform a given skill (Cartledge, 2005). To make social skills acquisition and instruction relevant, behaviors must be task analyzed. When teaching social skills, it is important to break down each skill as specifically as possible. The teacher will need to task analyze the behavior to all the subsequent subskills necessary to perform the skill. This can be difficult to do as many times general and special education teachers perform social skills without thinking about it, however, it is necessary in order to correctly teach the needed skill. See Table 9.1 for some examples of task analyzed behaviors.

Table 9.1
Task Analyses Examples

Responding to Corrective Feedback

• Face the person
• Make appropriate eye contact with the person
• Have an appropriate facial expression with the person
• Maintain straight body posture
• Use appropriate interpersonal space
• Use appropriate gestures
• Use appropriate voice volume
• Use appropriate timing of responses
• Acknowledge correction approach
• Apologize to the person
• State intention to rectify the situation
• Indicate intention to avoid making such an error in the future
• Listen attentively throughout the conversation
• Thank person for their feedback

Managing Conflict

• Face the person
• Make appropriate eye contact with the person
• Have an appropriate facial expression with the person
• Maintain straight body posture
• Use appropriate interpersonal space
• Use appropriate gestures
• Use appropriate voice volume
• Use appropriate timing of responses
• Make a request to resolve the conflict
• State appropriate goal
• Acknowledge what other person says
• Offer compromise appropriately to the other person
• Listen attentively throughout the conversation

When working with students on social skill development, general and special education teachers need to respond to a student's inability to perform a social skill exactly as they would to a student's inability to complete an academic task. If students do not know how to solicit teacher attention appropriately, they need to be actively and systematically instructed to signal for help, for example, by raising their hands. Situation-specific social skills instruction should focus on teaching behaviors perceived as functional by students and others with whom they interact. This process will take time and practice for all those involved. Clearly, to be successful in school, home, and work, it is important to exhibit positive social interactions. Positive social interactions are interactions that take place between peers that are positive in nature and successful for both children involved. These peer interactions are important because they lead to positive social and emotional development in children. Early positive social skills with peers can lead to the development of positive peer relationships, acceptance, and friendships. Although many children develop these positive social skills naturally, some children do not, especially those with disabilities

As indicated, social skills training is important to teach students appropriate social skills. Social skills training for adults with intellectual disabilities has received a substantial amount of attention over the last several decades (e.g., Chadsey-Rusch, 1992; Chadsey-Rusch & O'Reilly, 1992; Misra, 1992; O'Reilly, Lancioni, & Kierans, 2000). This training is very important since students with disabilities fail at home, school, and work because of improper social skills. Such attention seems warranted as deficits in social skills have been cited as a major factor in unsuccessful postschool adjustment with this population (Chadsey-Rusch, Rusch, & O'Reilly, 1991). For example, a lack of social compentence has been cited as a major reason for job separation with workers (Greenspan & Shoultz, 1981). Social skills training strategies that have typically been used with this population can be divided into two generic categories—external control strategies and problem-solving strategies (Gumpel, 1994). External control strategies consist of the following components: (a) a rationale for why the behavior is desirable; (b) an opportunity to observe examples of the behavior (i.e., modeling); (c) an opportunity to role-play the behavior; and (d) feedback regarding performance (e.g., Chadsey-Rusch, Karlan, & Rusch, 1984; Rusch & Menchetti, 1981). Several researchers have argued that external control strategies may not be effective in producing social skills that will generalize outside of the role-plays used in training (Gumpel, 1994; Park & Gaylord-Ross, 1989). That is, the targeted social behaviors may not be emitted when the person is confronted with a slightly different setting or with a problem that was not trained in the role-play situation. It is also argued that problem-solving interventions may offer an effective method for promoting generalization of social skills because the participant is taught a set of generic social rules that can be adapted to different social interactions (Gumpel, 1994). For example, the person may learn to use verbal rules to manage his/her social behavior following training.

Embedded in social skills training is problem-solving training. Problem-solving strategies have been examined to teach social skills to students with disabilities (O'Reilly et al., 2000; Park & Gaylord-Ross, 1989). These intervention strategies involve teaching the individual a generic set of verbal rules for social interactions in addition to the specific behaviors taught using external control strategies. General and special education teachers would need to prompt students to be able to (a) decode the situation (what is happening); (b) think of social skill options and identify the most appropriate social behavior for the social situation; (c) perform the social behavior; and (d) evaluate the effectiveness of the social behavior once it has been performed. This is an important process needed to make students successful in social situations. One of the most important issues when teaching youth social skills is determining whether targeted skills will enhance the quality of their lives. In addition to this aspect, general and special education teachers must also be thoroughly prepared to teach social skills. This is especially the case for general education teachers, who are likely to be the teachers who first encounter students with mild disabilities who present social skill deficits. These teachers can have the greatest impact on preventing or minimizing future behavior problems (Cartledge, 2005).

Generally, social skills instruction must occur in the classroom and, to the extent possible, be taught by the classroom teacher. Much of the instruction reported in the research literature shows students being taught in small groups outside the classroom and then returned to the same classroom conditions with no adaptations to either reinforce or heighten the opportunities for newly taught behaviors to occur. Newly acquired behaviors are not likely to persist under such conditions (Cartledge, 2005). Social skills instruction should not be treated as a fad. One option to teach social skills is to use a group setting which can be especially helpful to youngsters with social difficulties. Group treatment builds on three elements that have been shown to be effective: (a) creation of a social situation, (b) active participation in discussion, and (c) the use of group support (Shectman, 1993). Students with disabilities may learn from the behavior modeled by peers without disabilities, but that should not be the primary way students learn appropriate social skill, as we know direct teaching of social skills behavior is the most effective way to teach social skills.

Social Skills Training Packages

A barrier to significant social relationship development in the school can be timing. Due to schedules, students may not have enough opportunities to interact with others to practice and learn appropriate social skills. If students are to develop more in-depth relationships, then they need more time to develop the needed skills. Students need sufficient time to learn and practice social skills in order to get better at them. Classroom teachers can help students practice social skills by teaching these skills in the context of cooperative or work-based learning settings. Clearly, the consistent and effective use of acquired social skills is more likely to occur in schools that have a positive social atmosphere. Role playing is another helpful technique for engaging student interest and providing opportunities for practice and feedback. It allows students to take on roles, provide feedback to one another, practice new skills, and enables them to simulate a wide range of school, community, and workplace interactions (Bremer & Smith, 2004) in a safe classroom environment. When implementing role playing, however, it is critical to not only practice with feedback in the classroom, but also in real-world situations in the home, school, and community where general and special education teachers can see if students can generalize their social skills knowledge. Additionally, these teachers can provide unstructured time (e.g., recess) when students can practice their social skills with peers and experience feedback. Finally, general and special education professionals may want to consider a social skills training package. Considerations for selecting training packages include skills, training, setting, and logistics. See Table 9.2 for a description of each.

On the whole, it is important for students to avoid social mistakes, even though that is a part of life. Social mistakes will happen and students need to learn how to assess those mistakes and what to do differently the next time similar situations arise. While it is difficult to teach every situation, different situations can be practiced and discussed to get students to understand the evaluation process and to learn for better social skills in the future. General and special education teachers can make sure students leave high school with all the social skills they need to be successful. Bremer and Smith (2004) identified social skills needed by transition-aged students. See Table 9.3 for a list of these skills.

Table 9.2
Social Skills Training Packages Considerations

Characteristics	Considerations
Skills	General and special educators must make sure that social skills to be taught are (a) appropriate to group targeted for training (Sabornie & Beard, 1990); (b) reciprocal and produce positive responses from peers (Nelson, 1988); and (c) comprehensive enough to have meaning (that is, a great enough variety of social skills to be taught) (Sabornie & Beard, 1990).
Training	Training packages should (a) have a demonstrated research base (Sabornie & Beard, 1990); (b) provide necessary practice sessions and feedback opportunities for students (Schumaker & Hazel, 1984); and (c) consider the learning characteristics of the intended user group when considering instructional strategies.
Setting	Skills should (a) be taught in the most normalized setting possible; and (b) generalized to and maintained in a variety of environments.
Logistics	Packages should be (a) priced at a reasonable cost, and (b) user friendly for all those involved (Sabornie & Beard, 1990).

Table 9.3
Social Skills Needed by Transition-Aged Students

General Social Skills

- Being on time
- Using appropriate loudness and tone of voice
- Encouraging everyone to participate
- Learning and using peoples' names
- Looking at the person who is speaking
- Making eye contact with others when speaking
- Checking one's own understanding and asking appropriate questions
- Describing one's own feelings when appropriate
- Keeping remarks to an appropriate length
- Building on others' comments and ideas
- Supporting others, both verbally and nonverbally
- Asking for direction or assistance
- Participating appropriately in small talk
- Initiating and responding to humor

Continued on next page

Table 9.3 (continued)

Additional Social Skills Needed for Cooperative Learning

• Moving into work groups without disturbing others
• Staying with one's own group
• Keeping hands and feet to oneself
• Respecting time limits
• Setting group norms, such as "no put downs"
• Staying on the topic
• Offering to explain or clarify
• Criticizing ideas, not people
• Including everyone

Additional Social Skills Needed for Work Environments

• Giving and responding to instructions
• Greeting customers
• Responding to criticism

SOCIAL SKILLS AND COMMUNITY RESOURCES

Social skills are important to be successful in the community and workplace. Competence in using social skills will lead to positive perceptions of persons with disabilities in extended community settings such as postsecondary education, facilities, neighborhoods, and places of worship (Bremer & Smith, 2004). In addition to these settings, social interaction skills are an important part of positive leisure behavior. Most leisure behaviors require some degree of social competence. Many students with disabilities and/or illness lack adequate and appropriate social interaction skills and require direct intervention (Stumbo, 1995). Because many leisure situations require the presence of others and the results of these interactions produce pleasant experiences, "social interaction can be both a cause and effect of leisure involvement" (Iso-Ahola, 1980, p. 242). In other words, social interaction may be the primary purpose of a leisure activity or its byproduct. It follows, then, that an individual must have adequate and appropriate social skills in order to perform within a leisure or larger life context.

Teachers, parents, families, and schools should continue to look for available community resources to help students with disabilities become more independent and transition from high school to the community. Many times, there are government funded agencies that have programs and services available for individuals with transitional barriers. To locate these agencies, the phone book can be consulted as well as the local Chamber of Commerce. Those involved with the student should contact these agencies to see if their student/child qualifies for services. After a vocational assessment, the individual would be involved in developing a transition plan. This could happen while they are still in school, as an extension of the school program, or after the student has graduated. Possible services these agencies can provide include training and placement services. In *training services* individuals are trained to become independent. Students are trained on (a) social skills (e.g., asking for help and proper communication); (b) life skills (e.g., cooking, cleaning, and laundry); (c) independent living skills (e.g., money management, paying bills, and grocery shopping); and (d) work skills (e.g., following directions, assembly of materials, and being on time). Following an individual assessment and the development of a transition plan, specific training can be developed and implemented. Through classroom and workplace instruction (similar to a sheltered workshop format), training specialists can teach individual skills, give specific corrective feedback, and provide positive reinforcement to prepare individuals to move on to placement services. In *placement services*, individuals are taken through the process of getting and maintaining a job. They begin by going over the process of finding a job that fits their wants and skill levels and then do the application process. Next, the individual would go through the interview process, dress appropriately, and communicate effectively in a job interview. Upon getting a job, the individual might need some discussion on job roles and responsibilities as well as expectations of employment from the employer. In addition, some type of support such as job coaching might be provided. Job coaching would last until the individual can perform the job consistently and efficiently. Lastly, the agency might follow up every couple of weeks to see how the individual is progressing and maintaining his/her job. If unsuccessful, the whole process may begin again.

FINAL THOUGHTS

To be successful in and after high school, it is important for students with disabilities to have proper and appropriate social skills. Because social skills are so important, schools should consider some type of social skills instruction within the school's curriculum and daily operations. Adequate social skills need to be acquired while students are still enrolled in school and further supported and refined in postsecondary, community, and work settings since social mistakes will happen; students need to learn how to assess those mistakes and what to do differently the next time similar situations arise. Teachers, parents, families, and schools should look for available community resources to help students with disabilities become more independent and transition from high school to the community. Many times, there are government-funded agencies that have programs and services available for individuals with transitional barriers. Finally, we must recognize that students with disabilities need social skills instruction and this must be a part of the transitional plan and programming.

Chapter 10

TRANSPORTATION EDUCATION AND LEISURE/RECREATION OUTCOMES

Anne, a Caucasian female, is 16 years old and is currently a sophomore in high school. She has been diagnosed with a visual impairment and has limited vision in her right eye, with specific difficulties that include reading small printed materials, tracking written material on the board, movement in and out of school, participating in some social situations, and making friends. Academically, Anne does pretty well and is getting good grades falling in the middle of the class with regard to her peers. She does well when working independently with the proper supports but has more problems when not monitored as she chooses to not use her supports because she does not want to be different from the other students. She has difficulties maneuvering in school and in the community and does not participate in activities unless they are associated with the school.

Anne's case manager, Mr. Taylor, is concerned about how she will get around in the community after graduation if she does not use her supports. A positive note is that Anne's parents are very involved in her education and communicate with Mr. Taylor regularly. They attend all her IEP meetings and are very involved in her being successful. A direct concern of her parents is what Anne will do for leisure and how she will experience different activities so that she will know what she likes or dislikes. The task at hand is that Mr. Taylor wants to collaborate with Anne and her parents on ways to meet her transportation and leisure needs so she can be successful after graduation.

How might Mr. Taylor work with Anne and her parents to understand all of the options available to her after graduation? What could Mr. Taylor do to communicate clearly and effectively to Anne and her parents? This is the focus of this chapter. It is important for students with disabilities to be independent and enjoy life and part of that involves transportation and leisure activities. The ability to travel independently provides people with disabilities a vital key to achieving as much participation in society as they desire (Bourland, 1996). These are not skills students can necessarily pick up on their own. Any school preparing students with disabilities to live independently and hold employment must provide instruction on independent travel and use of community resources. Acquisition of travel skills should be coupled with acquisition of social, monetary, communication, and self-care skills that will be needed to participate fully in the workplace and community (MacWilliam, 1977). In fact, transportation and leisure are highly interconnected. All people need to be involved in recreation and leisure. Although acknowledged as a critical component to a person's well-being, leisure activities are not a priority in many transitional educational programs (Strand & Kreiner, 2001). Preparation for recreation and leisure pursuits for everyone needs to start early in the student's life. This is necessary to attain and maintain a level of physical and psychological wellness. However, this is a difficult task for transition-age students with disabilities, who, due to numerous factors, have not been actively involved with leisure activities or recreational programming.

TRAVEL TRAINING AND REQUIRED SKILLS

Travel training is short term, comprehensive, intensive instruction designed to teach students with disabilities how to travel safely and independently on public transportation. The goal of travel training is to teach students to travel independently to a regularly visited destination and back. The term "travel training" is often used generically to refer to a program that provides instruction in travel skills to individuals with any disability except visual impairments. Individuals who have a visual impairment receive travel training from orientation and mobility specialists. Travel trainers have the task of understanding how different disabilities affect a person's ability to travel independently; and they devise customized strategies to teach travel skills that address the specific needs of people with disabilities. Usually, specially trained personnel provide the travel training on a one-to-one basis. Students learn travel skills while following a particular route, generally to school or a worksite, and are taught the safest, most direct route. The travel trainer is responsible for making sure that students experience and understand the realities of public transportation, and learn the skills required for safe and independent travel (Bourland, 1996).

When planning travel training, students should be informed about possible barriers that may come into play. These could be in the form of architectural, ecological, or transportation barriers. *Architectural barriers* are man-made structures, such as buildings, walkways, and parks that are usable by people without disabilities but present obstacles for people with disabilities. These barriers limit mobility and often deprive individuals with disabilities from attending worthwhile leisure activities. *Ecological barriers* are physical obstacles that occur in the natural environment. Hills, trees, sand, rain, snow, and wind are some examples. The physical impact of such barriers is roughly the same as architectural barriers (Smith, 1985). *Transportation barriers* are those that prevent individuals with disabilities from enjoying recreational and leisure services because of the lack of usable and affordable methods of transportation. All of these barriers should be considered when planning and teaching travel training.

A good travel training program acknowledges a student's disabilities while making full use of a student's abilities (Bourland, 1996). Such a program focuses on what the student can do! There are some skills, however, that are quite necessary for successful travel. One important skill for travel is the ability to solicit aid from the public, usually for assistance in crossing streets and in locating unfamiliar destinations. In learning to solicit aid, the student must begin by role playing in the classroom and then in the community with the instructor simulating the public. Instructors should stress that the student must ask questions intelligibly succinctly, and courteously, and that they must also attend to the responses of those asked for guidance (MacWilliam, 1977). The general and special education teacher would first want to model appropriate behaviors, then move towards doing it together (guided practice) with corrective feedback, before finally letting the students to do it independently. Another important skill is the ability to give the correct amount of money if using public transportation. If traveling by car, taxi, or by public transportation systems such as a bus and subway, the student will need to pay for services. These services might enable students to go to work and come home, go to school or other training programs, visit friends, take care of daily needs such as grocery shopping, and enjoy recreational activities.

Process of Travel Training

When a student enters the school system, instruction can begin with activities that develop his/her sense of purposeful movement. Purposeful movement is the cognitive and physical ability to move safely and independently through the complex environments of school, home, and neighborhood, and includes such movements as negotiating stairs, using a telephone, boarding a bus, or crossing a street. As students progress through the school years, the various travel skills can be introduced and practiced routinely. Then, as students become young adults and are close to exiting the school system, explicit travel training can become part of their education and can form the basis of the transition from school transportation to public transportation. Most students who successfully complete a comprehensive travel training program along one route require little additional training to learn other routes and reach other destinations (Bourland, 1996).

When planning for travel training, there are some guidelines that are suggested to follow. First, most people enter travel training between the ages of 15 and 21. However, it may be appropriate for some children to be introduced to travel training at an earlier age. Next, travel training should occur at the time of day when a student will later be traveling independently, so that a trainer can assess the effectiveness with which the student handles the noise, varying light, crowds, fatigue, busy intersections, and empty streets associated with a particular route, and adjust travel training accordingly (Bourland, 1996). Obviously, there are some general skills that students should possess to participate in travel training. These skills include (a) an awareness of personal space and limits, (b) an awareness of environment, and (c) the ability to recognize and respond to danger. Other skills that are necessary for students to demonstrate include: (a) crossing streets safely (with and without traffic signals), (b) boarding the correct bus or subway, (c) recognizing and disembarking at the correct destination, (d) making decisions, (e) recognizing the need for assistance and requesting help from an appropriate source, (f) following directions, (g) recognizing and avoiding dangerous situations and obstacles, (h) maintaining appropriate behavior, (i) handling unexpected situations (such as rerouted buses or subways, or getting lost), and (j) dealing appropriately with strangers (see Bourland, 1996). It is important for students to have these skills as well as the ability to foresee possible risks associated with travel (Sauerburger, 2005). For instance, after the student has learned all the requisite street-crossing concepts and skills, he/she should be able to:

- Analyze the situation at hand (i.e., geometry and traffic control).
- Determine how and when to cross and if it is possible to do so (i.e., choose crossing strategy).
- Determine the possible risks of crossing with the chosen strategy.
- Reduce the risks as much as possible.
- Decide if the risks are acceptable enough to continue with your plan.
- Consider alternatives if the risks are not acceptable.

IMPORTANCE OF LEISURE AND RECREATION

Leisure and recreation are very important to students with disabilities and they are intricately linked to the overall success and satisfaction of these students. To accomplish the ultimate independence, planning and programmatic efforts should include a significant emphasis on recreation and leisure pursuits (Strand & Kreiner, 2001). Leisure provides the social linkages throughout the lifespan and can provide opportunities to gain social competencies through play, social groups, and inherent social interaction. Earlier, Russell (1996) suggested that leisure enables children to develop appropriate skills for social interaction, cultural ritual, personal autonomy, and sex roles. Teens, for example, use leisure to establish social networks and personal identities. In fact, leisure is often the sole link of older adults to the outside world and it is another method for developing social interaction and decision-making skills. Individuals with disabilities can experience the same growth through leisure as those without disabilities (Lord, 1997). Recreation and leisure are important in promoting health and wellness. Individuals with disabilities have less fitness and more health problems than the general population. These health problems could be reduced and fitness levels improved with a moderate increase in physical activity. When planning for leisure and recreation activities in the community, however, they must be planned with appropriate supports for lifelong experiences (Strand & Kreiner, 2001).

Some of the most common leisure activities for people with disabilities are watching television and listening to the radio (Hill, Rotegard, & Bruininks, 1984; Modell, Rider, & Menchetti, 1997). Many adults with disabilities do not participate in recreation activities (Sands & Kozleski, 1994) and are socially isolated from their communities (Kaye, 1997). It is obvious that we need to incorporate this facet of their future lives into transitional programming. Community sport, recreation, or leisure participation is one area in which transition planning can make a significant difference in a young person's quality of life. Harner and Heal (1993) indicated that people with disabilities who participated more regularly and had greater access to recreation and leisure activities were significantly more satisfied with their lives than were their peers. For example, bowling is an excellent community activity. With only minor modifications or accommodations, even children with the most severe disabilities can participate successfully. Bowling alleys offer a safe environment for all participants to access and achieve some level of success, and some even have the bumpers that fit in the gutters so everyone will be successful. Exposure and opportunities to experience leisure activities give students a knowledge base on which to determine preferences and choices. Many activities sound good or look good on paper, but being involved as an active participant can help to determine whether an activity is liked or disliked. In addition, recreation programs and leisure activities are excellent vehicles to provide students with opportunities to learn appropriate communication and social skills and activities (Strand & Kreiner, 2001).

PLANNING COMMUNITY-RELATED CURRICULUM
AND INSTRUCTIONS

To find out student interests and needs, a leisure assessment should be conducted. Typically, the types of leisure assessments utilized by schools and agencies are checklists of leisure activities, pictorial representations of leisure activities, or a verbal report. A method used frequently by teachers is direct observation. Through observation of students over a period of time, the watchful teacher can tell what each student prefers to do in his/her leisure time. Of course, this requires that the teacher allow free time and provide plenty of options from which students can choose during this free time. It may even require that the teacher or service provider teach the student how to make a decision regarding the choices. Another method for assessment in the leisure area is asking parents what their child likes to do in his/her free time. To provide a more valid method of assessing leisure activities for students, general and special educators should (a) select a variety of leisure activities for students to try, (b) make each activity fun, and (c) ask students questions about preferences from the assortment of checklists and pictorial questionnaires (Strand & Kreiner, 2001). It is essential that recreation professionals plan and implement programs that are accessible to people with disabilities and that the activities are student-centered.

Outdoor environments should be considered for students with disabilities, especially in planning instructional activities. These activities can promote physical fitness and health awareness and can also let students with disabilities experience nature and the great outdoors. These students should have the same opportunities and experiences as those without disabilities. Constraints to involvement in activities and the community, in general and in outdoor recreation in particular, tend to involve attributes and resources (Ross, 2001). The arguments are that the disability or resources will prevent students from participating and that they do not want to participate in outdoor activities. Interestingly, people with disabilities prefer the same kind of outdoor environments as do those without disabilities. Other negative arguments regarding the participation of persons with disabilities are that (a) they cannot attain a full range of benefits from outdoor recreation and adventure activities and programs because of their participation limitations, and (b) leisure service agencies and businesses cannot develop inclusive outdoor recreation and adventure opportunities due to accessibility and administrative and staffing barriers. The fact remains that persons with disabilities can enjoy all kinds of different activities after careful planning takes place (McAvoy, 2001).

For example, summer camps can be very beneficial (Fullerton, Brannan, & Arick, 2000). Summer programs when integrated with school programs, can increase outdoor recreation skills, improve sensitivity to the needs of other group members, and increase respect for nature among the participants with disabilities. City or county parks and recreation departments offer therapeutic recreation programs for individuals with disabilities as well. Other recreation program alternatives can be found in local resource guides, such as the yellow pages in phone books, which list youth organizations and centers, fitness centers, scouting organizations, church groups, park and recreation departments, and social service agencies. For some students, Special Olympics may be an option.

PLANNING THE CURRICULUM

When planning the leisure and recreation curriculum, an important factor to consider is the community. After all, for many students with disabilities, the community is where they will spend a lot of their time after graduation. When looking at secondary programs for students with disabilities, we must advocate for community-based curricula. To transition effectively into the community, it is crucial to implement community-based programs in addition to more traditional classroom-based programs. The ultimate goals for special education are adult interdependence and participation in community life, which can only be achieved by lifelong, true-to-life experiences. The current failure of special education graduates to achieve adult interdependence, especially in leisure and social settings, emphasizes the need for functional community-based programs. First, students need to have exposure to many diverse leisure experiences. In addition, they need to be provided with real-life, age-appropriate options, and opportunities to experience different activities. It is important that they experience many activities, try them out, and evaluate what they like or dislike (Strand & Kreiner, 2001). Leisure service professionals should provide social support to individuals with disabilities. This support should be reduced gradually as individuals gain more direct control of their life situations. Communication and social skills are keys to successful educational, work, and leisure experiences. Chalip, Thomas, and Voyle (1992) reported that persons who become more involved in sports and recreation developed larger networks of friends, received more social support, and were more likely to socialize with others.

When planning the curriculum, possible barriers that might prevent students with disabilities from full leisure participation must be considered. According to Smith (1985), these can be divided into three major categories: (a) intrinsic barriers which result from the individual's own limitations and may be associated with a physical, psychological, or cognitive disability; (b) environmental barriers which are composed of the many external forces that impose limitations upon the individuals with a disability; and (c) communication barriers which block interaction between the individuals and his or her social environment. See Table 10.1 for examples of each type of barrier.

Table 10.1
Possible Barriers to the Leisure Curriculum

	Intrinsic Barriers
Lack of Knowledge	Many people are not able to realize their maximum leisure functioning because they lack essential information. For example, knowledge of programs, facilities, and other recreation and leisure resources is needed in order to make informed choices.
Social Ineffectiveness	For many reasons, individuals with disabilities may have ineffective social skills. Parental overprotection and segregation from peers without disabilities are two or the most frequently mentioned reasons.
Health Problems	Most people with disabilities do not have significant health problems, but some types of disabilities do present recurring health problems.
Physical and Psychological Dependency	As any child grows into adulthood, there is a gradual progression toward physical and psychological independence. Unfortunately, many people who have disabilities do not achieve their potential for independent functioning. Some are genuinely limited by the effects of their disability, but others "learn" to be dependent in situations they have the capacity to control
	Environmental Barriers
Attitudinal Barriers	Of all the barriers to participation faced by individuals with disabilities, attitudinal barriers are probably the most limiting and difficult to overcome.
Economic Barriers	Even in times of low unemployment, job opportunities are more limited for people with disabilities; and when they do find employment, they frequently find themselves in low-paying positions with limited opportunity for advancement. The end result is less discretionary money to spend on leisure pursuits.

Continued on next page

Table 10.1 (continued)

Rule and Regulation Barriers	People with disabilities face many rules and regulations throughout history that have limited their ability to participate in all aspects of our society.
Barriers of Omission	The failure of society to provide for the needs of individuals with disabilities results in barriers of omission.
Communication Barriers	Communication barriers result from a reciprocal interaction between individuals with disabilities and their social environment. Both the sender and the receiver need to be active participants in the communication process.

TEACHING LEISURE AND RECREATION SKILLS

Once teachers, parents, and other stakeholders have established the student's needs, interests, and abilities with regard to viable community-based programs, teachers can then include functional transition skills within the curriculum (physical education or classroom). Functional transition skills are those skills that are needed for successful access and participation in a given activity (Modell & Valdez, 2002). Students must be provided with the skills necessary to spend their free time appropriately. Clearly, they would benefit from a rich body of experiences that provide opportunities for physical, recreational, and leisure activities.

General and special education teachers must provide students with skills that they will carry over into adulthood. They must make certain that students are learning functional leisure skills that can be exhibited in communities where the youth will be living. It is critical that students learn how to make choices and become self-confident in these choices. Recognizing that students have the right to change their mind is important. If educators complete their recreational assessments, provide opportunities for leisure activities, and have community-based supports, then the transition to adult life will be much easier. The key is to provide students with appropriate opportunities to be successful.

The more learning opportunities provided for students in the actual environment they will be performing, the more likely they will make the transition to adult activities successfully (Strand & Kreiner, 2001). Teaching students in the community is very important. Community leisure skill practice and regular contacts with the community foster successful outcomes for students with disabilities. Responsibilities in leisure community-based training include (a) teaching students appropriate leisure skills, (b) supervising student safety, (c) expecting students to act and interact appropriately, (d) monitoring student progress, (e) making sure that student wants to do the activity, (f) acting in a prudent manner in all situations, and (g) ensuring positive interactions with community members to change attitudes positively toward individuals with disabilities. Students, however, must learn the leisure skills and interact appropriately. In a community-based setting, it is important that the student wants to be there and to participate. He/she has the responsibility for saying "No" when he/she does not want to take part in the activity. Clearly, the student should be informed and understand there are consequences that go along with every choice (Strand & Kreiner, 2001). The recreation staff can help students practice appropriate social interaction scenarios via role playing before going on a field trip or outing. Leisure education is another method for developing social interaction and decision-making skills via a multitude of different situations and environments. The more opportunities the student gets out of the school environment and practice using available community resources, the smoother the transition will be (Strand & Kreiner, 2001). In a nutshell, leisure skills, like other skills, need to be taught.

FINAL THOUGHTS

It is important for students with disabilities to be independent and enjoy life. Part of this equation involves transportation and leisure activities. With regard to travel, students with disabilities need to travel safely and independently on public transportation. As educational professionals, we want our students to have the necessary skills to move about the community as well as the ability to make good choices for themselves. Leisure and recreation are very important to students with disabilities. Leisure provides the social linkages throughout the lifespan. It is often the sole link of older adults to the outside world and is another method for developing social interaction and decision-making skills. Community sport, recreation, and leisure participation is one area in which transition planning can make a significant difference in a young person's quality of life. Again, students must be taught appropriate leisure skills as well as given many leisure opportunities to find out what they enjoy doing with their free time. Collaborative efforts of family, friends, and teachers must be established to support individuals in the community leisure setting. For the leisure program to be successful, the student must be personally involved, and have fun and friends to accompany him or her in the leisure activity.

Chapter 11

INDEPENDENT LIVING OUTCOMES, RESIDENTIAL OPPORTUNITIES, GROUP HOMES, AND INTERMEDIATE CARE

Matt, a Caucasian male, is 18 years old and is currently a junior in high school. He has an educational diagnosis of a developmental disability, with an intelligence quotient (IQ) of 60 and difficulties in reading, mathematics, written expression, social skills, organizational skills, and adaptive behavior. He reads just above the second grade level, and is doing very well in math where he is working on money skills, banking, measurement (for cooking), and reading a clock. Matt can write his name, phone number, his address, and other personal information. Matt does a very nice job following directions, and he is a very hard worker. He has told his teacher several times that he wants to live independently after high school. Matt's parents are very supportive and communicate regularly with his teachers and case manager and they have also mentioned they would like to see him live independently after high school. Matt is working on being as independent as possible and focusing on making good choices and decisions as well as other skills necessary for the transition from high school to the real world of work. After high school, Matt's parents would like him to live as independently as possible, hold a job, and have appropriate social opportunities. Matt is very interested in living independently but is very open to other options as are his parents. Currently, he is interested in working with plants and trees as well as with animals as possible career choices.

Based on the above case, what are the different types of living arrangements and opportunities available and what program will best meet Matt's needs and fit best with his life-long aspirations? This chapter responds to this critical question. In recent years, the perspective that individuals with disabilities should be as independent as possible has been reflected notably in the way they are viewed in the society. The current notion is that they are capable of determining their own futures (Cameto, Levine, Wagner, & Marder, 2005). There has been an emphasis placed on including students with disabilities in their transition planning so that they have a say in what they will do and where they will live after high school. Studies have indicated that most adults with disabilities remain both single and living with their parents (Lindstrom & Benz, 2002; Sitlington & Frank, 1993). In addition, as youth leave high school, about one-quarter also leave their parents' homes, moving either to a postsecondary education setting, or to an apartment on their own or shared with roommates or a partner (Arnett, 2000). Sometimes, the lack of living options for students with disabilities is limited and that is why they live at home. One of the most discouraging barriers to successful transition for students as they move from school to adult living is the lack of satisfactory or satisfying residential alternatives. Residential settings that are most frequently considered as alternatives for these students include (a) independent living (alone or with a spouse, significant other, or roommates) in a house, mobile home, dormitory, or apartment; (b) supported living (alone or with someone else) in a house, mobile home, or apartment with periodic supervision; (c) living at home with one or both parents or other relatives with minimal to no supervision; (d) group home living with six to 10 other residents under minimal but continuous supervision; and (e) family care or foster home living with close and continuous supervision (Sitlington, Clark, & Kolstoe, 2000).

FUNDAMENTAL SKILLS NEEDED FOR
LIVING INDEPENDENTLY

When thinking about skills necessary to live independently, general and special education teachers need to remember that these skills often need to be taught to students with disabilities. It is easy to become focused on employment skill training in high school secondary transition programs and forget the importance of direct instruction in daily living or life skills. Clearly, the degree to which a person knows about and can perform daily living tasks is directly tied to how independent he/she is. Teachers and service providers owe it to their students and their students' families to provide instructional and learning experiences to prepare students to be as independent as possible. Daily living skills are important as they affect independence, but they also are important for positive emotional and social supports they provide. There are certain social problems that students with disabilities will experience if they cannot perform these skills effectively. Stares, embarrassing interactions, comments by observers, and questions from well-meaning but ignorant persons are typical. Competence in as many skills as possible will help individuals with disabilities to present themselves as confident and capable people willing to succeed (see Sitlington et al., 2000).

Independence

One aspect of independence involves the extent to which youth with disabilities are taking responsibility for their daily living needs. As youth mature, they often are expected to become more responsible for their own support within the household, such as fixing their own breakfast or lunch, straightening up their rooms or living areas, and doing their own laundry. In addition, most youth begin to function more independently outside of the home (e.g., by shopping for personal items). These kinds of daily living responsibilities can measure youths' competence and independence and how successful they will become in the community (Cameto et al., 2005). Financial responsibility is a key indicator of independence. As youth mature, they become able to earn, spend, and save money and become financially accountable for themselves. Obtaining a driver's license might help to increase independence of students. Most states allow 15-year-olds to apply for the learner's permits to enable young people to drive with an adult, and they permit 16-year olds to take a test to earn independent driving privileges. License requirements beyond passing written and driving tests vary from state to state (e.g., many require teens to take a formal driver education program), as do the privileges accorded teens of different ages (e.g., some states restrict hours that teens can drive and the passengers they can carry for the first six months of their driving career); and these contribute to their independence (Cameto et al., 2005).

Basic Skills

Students need to exhibit basic skills to be successful at living independently. The basic skills of listening and speaking are the foundations of peoples' interactions at home, in the neighborhood, at work, and in the community. It is important that transition education includes as much instruction and/or related services as needed for each individual to ensure that he/she can listen and speak effectively and independently in as many settings and situations as possible (Sitlington et al., 2000). Students with disabilities need to communicate effectively and this might entail lots of practice.

Functional Academic Skills

Functional academic skills for independent living involve reading, writing, and mathematical computation. Just as an inability to read, write, or solve math problems is not an insurmountable problem for getting and keeping a job, it is not an insurmountable problem for independent or interdependent living. Reading product labels, street signs, personal notes or letters, written instructions, and public notices are examples of common adult daily living tasks. Completing forms and writing personal notes or letters are written communication tasks requiring some academic skills in handwriting, spelling, and/or basic sentence construction. These are common adult activities, especially in employment and fulfilling the role of a friend or parent. Finally, counting, addition, subtraction, multiplication, division, and the use of fractions and decimals are common task demands in managing money, measuring, consumer problems, and job requirements. These skills are all important and if students cannot do them independently, siblings, parents, spouses, and sometimes children can help to provide them support for reading, writing, or math tasks (Sitlington et al., 2000).

Citizenship and Laws

To be a productive person in society, one must follow citizenship duties and laws. Citizenship duties and opportunities stem from three sources, namely: (a) what people must do or not do under the law, (b) what people are permitted to do under the law, and (c) what people are encouraged to do as good citizens to improve their communities. Students need to learn many different things to be good citizens. These include (a) specific information on laws directly related to good conduct as citizens, including information addressing misconceptions and misinformation that students might have learned from the media, family members, or peers who are not well-informed; (b) specific information on accessing assistance from law enforcement officers, reporting crimes, what it means to testify in court, and some understanding of penalties that are commonly associated with criminal behavior; (c) specific knowledge and skills for obtaining information through accessing public records, public meetings, public services (e.g., libraries, museums, parks, and recreation) and public and private assistance agencies (e.g., legal aid, public health, mental health, Planned Parenthood, and hotlines for suicide, substance abuse, and child abuse); and (d) specific information on alternatives for community contributions, including volunteering for organizations and agencies, self-initiated activities for the welfare of the neighborhood and others (e.g., recycling and neighborhood clean-up), and charitable giving (see Sitlington et al., 2000). If students can learn about these facets of citizenship, they will be more successful in their community.

Health and Safety Issues

To be independent, students need to take care of themselves. They need knowledge about good nutrition, rest, and exercise. Adolescents do not always recognize the importance of knowing about and following through with health information and fitness and the positive impact it has on mental health. As Sitlington et al. (2000) noted, exercise has highly beneficial effects in reducing stress, changing self-image, and increasing self-confidence. Some health and safety concerns students might need instruction on include (a) preventing colds and other contagious conditions; and (b) prenatal nutrition and avoidance of tobacco, alcohol, and harmful drugs, personal hygiene, immunizations, healthy sleep patterns, preventing infections, and use of over-the-counter and prescription medications.

CENTERS FOR INDEPENDENT LIVING

Essentially, independent living is living just like everyone: else having opportunities to make decisions that affect one's life, being able to pursue activities of one's own choosing, and limited only in the same ways that anyone else is limited (Kailes, 2006). Independent living does not mean that a person wants to do everything by himself/herself without help or that he/she wants to live in isolation (Independent Living Institute, 2006); it means that a person wants to control his/her own life. Independent living should not be defined in terms of living on one's own, being employed in jobs, or having an active social life. It has to do with self-determination, having the right and the opportunity to pursue a course of action, and having the freedom to fail and to learn from one's failures like everybody else (Kailes, 2006). In fact, independent living is a philosophy and movement of people with disabilities being able to work for self-determination, equal opportunities, and self-respect (see Independent Living Institute, 2006).

Independent Living Centers

Independent living centers are unique in that they are run by people with disabilities who themselves have been successful in establishing independent lives. These people have both training and the personal experience to know exactly what is needed to live independently. In addition, they have a deep commitment in assisting other people with disabilities in becoming more independent. Centers typically serve a wide variety of disability groups, including people with mobility impairments (which may be caused by spinal cord injury, amputation, neuromuscular disease, and cerebral palsy) as well, as people who have visual impairments, hearing impairments, mental retardation, mental illness, traumatic brain injury, and many other disabilities (Kailes, 2006).

The Rehabilitation Act of 1973 (PL 93–112) and ensuing amendments serve as the framework for the federally funded independent living program that supports what has become a national network of centers for independent living (CILs). At least, one CIL is located in each state, the District of Columbia, the U.S.A. Virgin Islands, Puerto Rico, and American Samoa. The CIL program annually provides hundreds of thousands of individuals who have severe disabilities with direct services that include, but are not limited to, information and referral, independent living skills training, peer counseling and mentorship, and consumer advocacy (Frieden, Richards, Cole, & Bailey, 1979). Each CIL is mandated to provide a well-defined group of core services and designed to provide programs and deliver services that generally meet the needs of most disability groups, while attempting to address the specific demographic and geographic characteristics of its region (Wilson, 1998). CILs are legislatively defined as consumer-controlled, community-based, cross-disability, nonresidential, and private nonprofit agencies. They are designated and operated within local communities, primarily by individuals with disabilities, and provide an array of independent living services (The Rehabilitation Act of 1973). Centers offer a wide variety of services. With regard to information and referral, these centers maintain comprehensive information files in their communities on accessible housing, employment opportunities, transportation, interpreters (for people with hearing impairments), readers (for people with visual impairments), rosters of persons available to serve as personal care attendants, and many other services. These centers also provide training courses to help people with disabilities gain skills that would enable them to live more independently. Specifically, these courses may include managing a personal budget, dealing with insensitive and discriminatory behavior by members of the general public, using various public transportation systems, and many other relevant and worthwhile subjects (Kailes, 2006).

Characteristics of high quality CILs include (a) strong leadership with a good community connection; (b) flexibility in the provision of extended services; (c) diverse, resourceful staff and volunteer corps; (d) demonstrated appreciation for strong collaborative partnerships with community stakeholders; and (e) sound understanding and consideration of community-specific needs (Wilson, 1998). In contrast to many community-based organizations that develop programs and provide support services to people with disabilities, CILs model consumer control. That is, they delegate power and authority within their organizational structure. For the most part, people with disabilities hold leadership and decision-making positions; get intricately involved in the program planning process; and are the primary providers of training, counseling, and all other direct services offered by CILs. By design, CILs are service organizations that encourage people who themselves have been successful at establishing independent, self-sufficient lives to assist others with disabilities to do the same. Most of the staff have relevant training and personal experience, know exactly what is required to live independently, and have a true commitment to sharing their knowledge and experience with others as they serve as role models and mentors (Wilson, 1998). CILs have realized that not only is their administrative structure and community-based posture conducive to the provision of transition support services, they also provide appropriate services for youth in transition (Wilson, 1998). To locate the nearest center, individuals must (a) look in the local telephone directory under social services, (b) try both the regular and the yellow pages, (c) contact the main office of the state vocational rehabilitation agency (the local public librarian should help to obtain the address and telephone number), and (d) request that the person responsible for overseeing the agency's independent living program provide information on centers in the respective state. In addition, individuals may contact the Rehabilitation Services Administration's Office of Independent Living (330 C Street, S.W., Switzer Bldg., Washington, D.C. 20202, 202–732–1400). Staff members will have a listing of the approximately 150 centers which it funds (Kailes, 2006).

On the whole, besides being able to hold a job and live independently, independent living centers address personal-social issues. Counseling, whether peer or professional, is at the heart of the services of agencies like this and continually focuses on learning to take control over one's life (emotionally, socially, occupationally, and functionally at home and in the community). Even the supports given in housing, transportation, interpreting (for the deaf), legal problems, reading, attendant care, and training in independent living are designed to increase self-confidence and minimize dependence on others. Two groups of students with disabilities that appear to need mental health services more than other groups are those who are classified as having emotional/behavior disorders or mild mental retardation (Sitlington et al., 2000). This should be a serious consideration when working with these two groups and other students with disabilities as well. Clearly, independent living centers offer many different services depending on the specific needs of their consumers and lack of availability elsewhere in the community. Among the most frequently provided services are community education and other public information services, home modifications, recreational activities, and equipment repairs (Kailes, 2006). The road to independence for adolescents also involves the development of a variety of self-determination skills, including persisting with tasks to completion and knowing how and when to advocate for oneself (Cameto et al., 2005). The objective is to explore options and to solve problems that sometimes occur for people with disabilities. For example, experiencing changes in living arrangements, making adjustments to a newly acquired disability, or learning to use community services more effectively would be some options students could explore (Kailes, 2006). Lastly, centers may provide advocacy services, namely: (a) *consumer advocacy* which involves center staff working with persons with disabilities to obtain necessary support services from other agencies in the community, and (b) *community advocacy* which involves center staff, board members, and volunteers initiating activities to make changes in the community that make it easier for all persons with disabilities to live more independently (see Kailes, 2006).

RESIDENCY IN GROUP HOMES

A group home is an option for students with disabilities. A group home is a dwelling for four to six people that is, wherever possible, located in a residential neighborhood, or in an area zoned residential by the local government authority. The location is usually accessible to services and supports meeting client needs, including family or social support, transport, commercial services, education, medical, employment and recreational facilities (Department of Ageing, Disability, & Home Care, 2006). Group homes are for people over the age of 18 who have an intellectual disability with moderate to high support needs. To be eligible, people must have an independent assessment, which determines their level of support needs. These homes usually provide 24-hour support to those who reside there and are staffed by Residential Support Workers. The staffing level is in accordance with the assessed need of the group of clients in the Group Home (see Department of Ageing, Disability, & Home Care, 2006). For example, more severe client needs would require more staff to meet those needs. See Table 11.1 for characteristics of typical group homes (see Department of Ageing, Disability, & Home Care, 2006).

Table 11.1
Characteristics of Group Homes

Group Homes have:

• 4 to 6 bedrooms, to allow clients to have individual bedrooms
• Sufficient outdoor recreational and leisure space
• Adequate space for clients, staff (including some office capacity), and provision for visitors

Group Homes provide:

• Small-group supported accommodation in a community setting
• Supports for clients to carry out essential daily living activities
• Support and assistance for people who even with support cannot reside independently or with their family
• Community opportunities for residents to participate in the community, who, without support would not be able to do so

Who has priority of access?

• People with complex multiple needs
• People with assessed complex challenging behavior
• People who are at risk of entering a more restrictive option and/or whose career is likely to be at risk unless entry into the service is facilitated
• People who are homeless or who are at risk of becoming homeless

---

Staff in group homes work to support clients by teaching them and working with them on many different skills. These skills include general self-care, skills development, living with a group, accessing and utilizing community resources, the art of decision making, and the management of finances. Some clients in group homes have learner outcomes that focus on respect, healthy diet, personal hygiene, accessibility to medical services, safe environment, and proper selection and maintenance of clothing. But, how effective are group homes? Hatton, Emerson, Robertson, and Henderson (1995) found that specialized group homes for people with intellectual disabilities who also had sensory impairments achieved better results than "ordinary" homes in which people with comparable needs lived with other people with intellectual disabilities. Emerson, Beasley, Offord, and Mansell (1992) noted that homes which grouped people who had very severe challenging behaviors achieved no improvement in client outcomes over institutional care. As Mansell (1995) discovered, specialized placements in "mixed" homes achieved better results than grouped settings. When considering this option, teachers, parents, and students should make sure that the needs of the student and services provided by the group home are matched as closely as possible for the best possible outcomes.

INTERMEDIATE CARE FACILITY

Intermediate Care Facilities (ICFs) are for individuals who are developmentally disabled. The main goal of these facilities is to nurture residents and encourage them to be as independent as possible. The goal of an ICF is to help residents to live full and active lives, and each ICF has a unique atmosphere for residents requiring different levels of care. ICFs are designed for individuals with chronic conditions who are unable to live independently but do not need constant intensive care. They provide supportive care and nursing supervision under medical direction 24 hours per day, yet it is not a nursing home. Students in ICFs frequently need rehabilitation therapy to enable them to return to a home setting or regain or retain as many functions of daily living as possible. In some cases, these students need a full range of medical, social, recreational, and support services. There are two kinds of ICFs: one is for students with developmental disabilities that tends to provides 24-hour personal care, and developmental and supportive health services. The other is the habilitative ICF that tends to have a capacity of 4 to 15 beds and provides 24-hour personal care, developmental and supportive health services to 15 or fewer persons with developmental disabilities who have intermittent recurring needs for nursing services.

EVALUATING LIVING AND RESIDENTIAL CENTERS

Different living and residential centers should be evaluated before a decision is made for students. The programs of each center reflects the quality of that center. These programs can be evaluated from the perspectives of (a) *accessibility* (e.g., getting around the facility, parking, and reaching staff); (b) *process measures* (how staff delivers services to consumers and how they provide advocacy to their community); (c) *philosophy* (what is philosophy of facility and does it match goals/expectations); (d) *services provided* (e.g., television, telephone, proper cabinet height, and daily living skills instruction); (e) *variations in service* (to meet the different needs of different people); (f) *advocacy* (e.g., transportation, enforcement of civil rights laws, education, and youth transition); (g) *relationships with other agencies* (cross-training of different programs and services available to clients); (h) *consumer satisfaction* (how happy are consumers with services); (i) *outcomes* (community changes that have occurred); (j) *acquisition of financial resources* (e.g., raising funds to support staff and services); and (k) *evaluation and monitoring* (i.e., how the agency evaluates and monitors consumers, staff, and services). There will probably not be an available program that has everything, but teachers, parent(s), and the student (when appropriate) should consider all these aspects when looking into a possible program after high school.

To address accessibility issues for each individual, the following should be taken into serious considerations (see Disability Rights Commission, 2006):

- Accessible rooms for wheelchair users or those with mobility difficulties.
- Full access to leisure and other facilities.
- Rooms that are accessible and with a range of accommodations so that students can both choose the style of accommodation they prefer, and live near their friends.
- Larger rooms for those with additional technology.
- Plenty of wall outlets for students using additional technology.
- Ensuring televisions in common rooms have Teletext.
- Contrasting paint colors for doors and corridors.
- Car parking spaces.

According to the Disability Rights Commission, individual considerations are necessary ingredients for healthy home living. Following are important considerations:

- Installation of hoists.
- Provision of private fridge to store drugs.
- Braille markings on microwaves.

- Extra shelving for Braille materials.
- Flashing lights or other alerts for deaf/hard of hearing students.
- Special space for an assistance dog.
- Adaptations to fire and other emergency procedures.
- Training for staff and other students in emergencies (e.g., someone having a seizure).

CHOOSING THE RIGHT RESIDENTIAL PROGRAM

Each decision should be made on an individual basis and must take into consideration the disability, the needed services and support, and the goals and aspirations of the student and parent(s). Many times the problem that prevents individuals with disabilities from achieving independence and control, of their own self-directed lives within their own communities, lies within the attitudinal and physical environments in which they live (Independent Living Institute, 2006). It is very important to choose the right option for each student. For many Americans with disabilities, however, barriers in their communities take away or severely limit their choices. These barriers may be obvious, such as lack of ramped entrances for people who use wheelchairs, lack of interpreters or captioning for people with hearing impairments, or lack of brailed or taped copies of printed material for people who have visual impairments. One barrier that is frequently less obvious but can be even more limiting is low expectation about things people with disabilities can do and achieve (Kailes, 2006). When looking at different programs, it is important to physically go to the place that one is considering as well as speak with staff and current clients. In addition, it is critical to look at (a) *licensure* (Does the facility have a current license?); (b) *medical needs* (Can the medical needs of the student be met and does the program have the necessary health care?); (c) *psychological services* (Are proper psychological services provided?); (d) *physical and occupational therapy* (Are these services provided and are proper records kept?); (e) *nursing services* (Is a nurse available when needed and is health care training provided?); (f) *social services* (Are family coping and individual social functioning services provided?); (g) *speech pathology and audiology services* (Are qualified speech pathologists and audiological services accessible?); (h) *pharmacy* (Does the facility have a provision for emergency pharmacy services?); (i) *fire safety* (Are state and local fire codes met and are fire drills frequently conducted?); (j) *proper staffing* (Does the staff show interest in, affection, and respect for each individual resident and are there the appropriate numbers of staff given the numbers of clients?); (k) *resident rights* (Are individuals given choices and provided sufficient community experiences, vocational skills training, and recreational and leisure activities?); (l) *food options* (Are individuals receiving three nutritious meals a day and is all food stored and served properly?); and (m) *building and ground issues* (Is the facility clean, comfortable, and provided with safety features such s grab bars on toilets and slip resistant surfaces in tubs and showers?) (New Mexico Health Care Association, 2002).

FINAL THOUGHTS

When planning with students and families for life after high school, one needs to consider employment, transportation, leisure and recreation, and the type of living arrangement. Options for residential settings that are most frequently considered as alternatives for students with disabilities include (a) independent living (alone or with a spouse, significant other, or roommates) in a house, mobile home, dormitory, or apartment; (b) supported living (alone or with someone else) in a house, mobile home, or apartment with periodic supervision; (c) living at home with one or both parents or other relatives with minimal to no supervision; (d) group home living with six to 10 other residents under minimal but continuous supervision; and (e) family care or foster home living with close and continuous supervision (see Sitlington et al., 2000). Negative to skeptical attitudes about young persons with disabilities living independently come not only from community neighborhoods, landlords, or apartment managers, but also from parents, professionals, and sometimes the individuals with disabilities themselves. This is a concern and should be dealt with through instruction in vocational-based programs in the school as well as community-based programs. Proactive efforts must be made to provide persons with disabilities with appropriate opportunities to live independently and maximize their fullest potential in the community outside the school.

Chapter 12

POSTSECONDARY EDUCATION OUTCOMES

Anastasia, an African American female, is 17 years old and is a sophomore in high school. She has an educational diagnosis of learning disability, with specific difficulties in reading comprehension, mathematical skills, and time management. She has the ability to complete most of her assignments, but quite often does not get her work finished on time. When she works in a group, her work gets turned in on time; but when working independently, she has most of her problems. Anastasia can read just below grade level, but has difficulty understanding what she reads. She can apply her math skills well but has problems remembering the basic facts. After high school, Anastasia wants to attend some post-secondary option. She and her parents have expressed an interest in college at previous IEP meetings. Her parents are very supportive and communicate regularly with her teachers and case manager and try to be as supportive as they can, but they also know that she needs to learn to advocate effectively for herself. She would like to pursue a degree in nursing or some other health-related field but realizes this may not be reasonable. Anastasia and her family are open to what type of program would best fit her needs with proper supports. Anastasia has experience working with children as a babysitter and has also volunteered at the local hospital on weekends.

Based on the above case, two questions are critical. What type of postsecondary education program would best fit Anastasia's needs and what kinds of supports and accommodations could she receive in this type of setting? This chapter responds to these questions. As the American economy becomes increasingly more knowledge based, attaining a postsecondary education appears more important than ever. Whereas only 20 percent of workers needed at least some college for their jobs in 1959, by 2000 that number had increased to 56 percent (Carnevale & Fry, 2000), and it is still growing. Postsecondary education then is very important for everyone including students with disabilities. Formal postsecondary training alternatives include college, postsecondary vocational and technical schools, adult education, specialized training in the military, and job training and apprentice programs. For students to be successful after high school, they must have the necessary skills to transition to these different environments. Transitions, by nature, are difficult and require time for adjustment and efforts to minimize the impact of the problems that will inevitably be confronted. Transitioning from high school to higher education is particularly difficult for students with disabilities (Madaus, 2005). Effective transitions are possible when proper supports are in place. In fact, Halpern, Yovanoff, Doren, and Benz (1995) found that students with disabilities who had engaged in some formal transition planning were more likely to pursue postsecondary education than those who had not. If students are to complete high school and move on to some sort of postsecondary option, they must be provided with proper supports and instruction while at the same time including their parents and families in this process.

COLLEGES AND CAREER EDUCATION

Students with disabilities do attend college; however, they reach college settings at a significantly lower rate than their peers without disabilities (Wagner, Newman, Cameto, Garza, & Levine 2005). In a National Organization on Disability Study (1998), one-third of people with disabilities report encountering key barriers to obtaining the education and training they desire. General and special education teachers must prepare their students and families through training and instruction about these barriers. These barriers include a lack of (a) awareness by students, families, and school staff of postsecondary education opportunities and requirements; (b) support to meet postsecondary education requirements; and (c) students' ability to identify their own disabilities, recognize accommodation needs, and use self-advocacy skills necessary to access these accommodations (National Council on Disability, 2000). Ensuring that students with disabilities have access and participate fully in postsecondary education is one of the key challenges in secondary education transition for such students (National Center on Secondary Education and Transition, 2003). As the American economy becomes increasingly knowledge based, attaining a postsecondary education becomes more critical than ever (Carnevale & Desrochers, 2003); and teachers, parents, and other school personnel need to prepare students with disabilities accordingly.

Postsecondary School Experiences

After high school, the student with a disability will need to transition to some other placement/option. The transition team along with students and their parents should decide what post-secondary option would be the best fit. There are many possible options for students with disabilities. Postsecondary education includes (a) postsecondary vocational and technical education programs, (b) a two-year junior or community college, (c) a four-year college or university, (d) adult education, (e) apprenticeships, (f) the military, and (g) taking courses towards a GED (Newman, 2005).

Postsecondary Vocational and Technical Education Programs

Postsecondary vocational and technical education programs include vocational and technical schools (public and private) and vocational programs in junior and community colleges. These programs usually last for two years and result in a certificate or an associate's degree, depending on the area. As a result of 1973 Section 504 of the Vocational Rehabilitation Act (PL 93–112) and the Americans with Disabilities Act of 1990 (PL 101–336), most postsecondary vocational programs have developed support services similar to those found in high schools, colleges, and universities (Clark & Kolstoe, 1995) to provide students with disabilities with the resources they will need to be successful.

College and University Programs

College and university programs are sometimes options. These institutions are attended to acquire a four-year degree. Availability of college and university programs is not as significant a problem as accessibility. Some campuses are still partially inaccessible architecturally and some are simply difficult for mobility because of the terrain. Curb cuts, elevators, accessible restrooms and classrooms, lowered drinking fountains, and door-opening mechanisms are important for those with mobility impairments to make a campus more accessible. Accessibility, however, is more than an architectural issue. Program accessibility is also important, and it is at this level that some students with disabilities have the most difficulty, but legislation has helped to give access to these students. Getting students properly prepared for this option is critical as prior school-related experiences have strong associations with enrollment in two- or four-year colleges. In terms of more specific recommendations to assist the transition into colleges and universities, high schools can offer workshops to help students understand that fewer services will be available to them in these institutions of higher education. In these workshops, the school district's transition specialist can play a significant role by providing information to students about services available in local colleges (Eckes & Ochoa, 2005). Another recommendation is to have a guest speaker from a college visit the high school to answer questions about transition. Secondary schools can also benefit from enlisting parental participation and gradually shaping how parents participate in their child's education.

Adult Education

Another option for students with disabilities is adult education. Most adult education programs do not have a strong vocational education component. Some offer courses in auto mechanics, carpentry, or welding; but these and similar courses are designed more for home maintenance and repairs or for hobby and leisure activities. Training in secretarial and office procedures, computer operation, and bookkeeping are the most common and do provide some options; but they are very limited in appeal. It would be important to look for adult education programs that are highly comprehensive and can provide enough alternatives to make adult education a good alternative for postsecondary vocational training. Adult education course offerings are typically subject to the request of potential students and that is a limitation as there needs to be a sufficient enrollment in the adult education courses to justify teaching them.

Apprenticeships

Apprenticeship training is a job training alternative that has eluded persons with disabilities (Hasazi & Cobb, 1987) in spite of the fact that the Department of Labor requires equal access and opportunity to the program by any participating employer. Labor unions have managed to gain control over most apprenticeship programs because most trainings occur in the construction trades, metalworking, and printing which are trades that unions have a history of involvement. As a result, local union representatives must be contacted for the possibility of an apprenticeship for students.

Military Training

Another option is military training. Military training opportunities go beyond vocational and technical training in skill fields to include college credit for certain career areas. Many individuals with disabilities either currently work for, or have worked for, the U.S. Military in one branch or another, as part of the civilian workforce. In addition, opportunities are available for students with disabilities going in as enlisted or as a commissioned officer as well (Rabbe, Silts-Scott, Santa, & Sweringen, 2001). Physical and mental selection criteria exclude many high school youths who see the military as one way of getting some vocational training and as a magic carpet out of their home and community environments; however, there are few who are able to pass both physical and mental requirements and enlist in a branch of military service. Once in the military, students may qualify for or choose training in a variety of occupational areas that support the overall military mission. This training might provide them with skills for possible employment when they return to civilian life.

Parental Involvement

As is the case for postsecondary school participation, parents' expectations can be a powerful influence on the employment options, experiences, and outcomes of youth as they become young adults (Osgood, Foster, Flanagan, & Ruth, 2005). Clearly, students will benefit if secondary schools and parents work to empower students to take on a leading role in advocating for themselves. Being aware of parents' postsecondary education expectations is important because they can help shape students' attitudes and behaviors toward their schooling. High educational expectations can encourage the educational attainments of youth (Catsambis, 2002; Patrikakou, 2004) and parents' expectations for youth with disabilities have been shown to be powerfully related to the youth's accomplishments in multiple domains, including postsecondary education (Wagner, Blackorby, Cameto, & Newman, 1993). It is important for parents to be empowered to understand the "expectations game." Rather than have high or low expectations, it is critical that they have *realistic expectations* to avoid overestimation or underestimation which in the long run lead to disappointments.

SUPPORT SERVICES AT POSTSECONDARY LEVELS

When students leave high school, their education is no longer covered under the IDEA umbrella, but instead is under two civil rights laws: Section 504 of the Rehabilitation Act and the Americans with Disabilities Act (ADA) (Stodden, Jones, & Chang, 2002; Wolanin & Steele, 2004). Postsecondary students with disabilities are not entitled to a free appropriate public education, as in high school, nor is there a mandatory individualized education program (IEP) process to identify and provide for the supports they may need to succeed in school (Office for Civil Rights, 2004). If they have been receiving rehabilitation services as part of their transition plans, however, they can continue to receive them. These supports may be the one thing that helps them to succeed in different environments. Receiving appropriate supports and accommodations can be critical to the postsecondary school success and retention of those who are enrolled in postsecondary school programs (Stodden & Dowrick, 2000; Stodden et al., 2002). To provide support services, colleges and universities must require documentation of a disability (i.e., results of tests indicating the presence of a disability) and having an IEP or Section 504 plan in high school is not enough documentation to obtain services at this level. In order to receive accommodations at this level, students entering postsecondary programs will need to present current assessment data or possibly be assessed at college level (Taymans & West, 2001).

The transition from a high school resource situation to a college campus with no direct services can be devastating for even the brightest student with disabilities. College professors generally expect a high degree of independence and academic excellence, which may be beyond the incoming students who have spent their high school years with special education teachers who have tutored them in the academic subjects, administered classroom tests orally, and carefully monitored academic progress (Dexter, 1982). In high school, "the burden is on the school to find and serve the student . . . in higher education the burden is on the student . . . to find the appropriate services and navigate through (their) education" (Wolanin & Steele, 2004, p.27). Growth in the number of students with disabilities entering higher education has fueled a need for postsecondary personnel who work to ensure these students are provided equal educational opportunities (Dukes & Shaw, 1999). Disability support services at colleges and universities play an important role in facilitating access of students with disabilities to higher education (Szymanski, Hewitt, Watson, & Swett, 1999). Virtually all colleges, community colleges, and universities have supportive services of some type already in existence on their campuses, such as reading clinics, instructional centers, or basic skill centers (Cordoni, 1982). Some other services, offered on an individualized basis, and which vary from campus to campus include (a) campus orientation, (b) mobility training, (c) academic advisement and planning, (d) career counseling, (e) campus adaptive transportation, (f) registration assistance, (g) assistive technology, (h) volunteer note-taking, and (i) sign-language interpreting.

Most colleges and universities have counseling centers or mental health services to assist all students with personal adjustment problems. Individual and group counseling in these programs are not only available but are accessible to any student at no cost. In addition, residential programs administered by colleges offer a variety of opportunities for personal-social development through group meetings to solve common problems, special guest speakers on adjustment to college life, and noncredit workshops or seminars on special topics of concern to college-age students. Some of the special topics focus on drinking problems, recreational drug use, sexuality, suicide, personal crisis, or special health-related topic such as AIDS (Clark & Kolstoe, 1995). These services are provided to students; however, it is up to the student to access these services as needed. Most importantly, virtually all college programs have tutoring services available for students if they need them. While colleges and universities usually have education programs they can tap for tutors, institutions that do not have education programs (i.e., community colleges) can have a problem in this area (Cordoni, 1982). Again, if students need help, it is up to them to access the help they need versus in high school where the help may have automatically been provided to them.

College and university programs typically have study centers to help students to be acquainted with (a) problem-solving skills, (b) study skills (e.g., note-taking, reading, and test-taking), (c) self-advocacy skills (interacting with faculty, staff, and other students to obtain support services necessary for learning needs), and (d) self-management skills (e.g., planning academic and personal schedules and developing and maintaining academic and personal routines)(University of Washington, 2001). These study centers sometimes focus on the relationship of time in and out of classes. A general rule of the thumb for the average college student is to plan on a minimum of two hours outside of class for every hour in class. Managing one's time is critical to be successful and to get everything completed in a timely fashion. It is important for students to take breaks from studying even if they consist only of stretching, walking down the hall, or just getting up from the desk for mental and physical reasons. As students keep a daily record of the amount of time they need to complete each assignment, they soon develop the ability to project how much time they will need on future assignments (Dexter, 1982). These are all skills that can be worked on during the transition program in high school, but that will also be provided for students in a college or university as they need them.

AVAILABILITY OF FINANCIAL AIDS
AT POSTSECONDARY LEVELS

Life in college is full of expenses, expected and unexpected. There are resources to assist with and, in some cases, fully cover costs such as tuition, books, rent, lab fees, assistive technology, and application fees. Resources are not the same at each postsecondary institution, so some research may be necessary. Financial aid is designed to help individuals meet their educational expenses when their own resources are not sufficient to pay for all the costs of attendance (e.g., tuition, room and board, books, transportation, campus activities). Students should apply for financial aid through the financial aid office of the institution that they plan to attend (Gardner & Hartman, 1997). Financial aid is based upon a partnership between the student, parents, postsecondary educational institutions, state and federal government, and available private resources. For the student with a disability, the partnership may be extended to include a Vocational Rehabilitation Agency and the Social Security Administration. The federal government is the single largest source of financial assistance for postsecondary education (by comparison, grants and scholarships from private sources account for less than two percent of all college financial aid). Federal financial aid is made up of grants (which do not need to be repaid), loans (which must be repaid, with interest), and work-study programs (Gardner, 2000). Because so much financial aid is awarded as loan money, students and their families should be careful not to bite off more loan debt than they can comfortably handle.

Awareness of Financial Need

Most federal financial aid is awarded on the basis of the applicant's financial need. Financial need is formulated by comparing the student's educational expenses with the amount of money the student's family can be expected to contribute. The expected family contribution is determined by a formula that considers the family's income and assets, size, and basic living expenses (Gardner, 2000). In addition, the student with a disability is often faced with additional expenses not incurred by other students. These may include (a) transportation necessary to pursue an academic program, if regular transportation is not accessible; (b) expenses of services for personal use of study, such as readers, interpreters, note-takers, or personal care attendants; (c) medical expenses relating directly to the individual's disability that are not covered by insurance; and (d) special equipment (related to the disability) and its maintenance (Gardner & Hartman, 1997). Students must inform the Office of Disability Support Services and/or Financial

Aid Office to determine disability-related expenses that may previously have been covered by the family budget. These may include food and veterinary bills for guide dogs, batteries for hearing aids and a Telecommunication Device for the Deaf (TDD) [now called Typed Text or TTY], or the cost of recruiting and training readers or personal care attendants (Gardner & Hartman, 1997). Some of the special equipment and support services may also be available at the post-secondary institution itself.

Application for Financial Aid

The Free Application for Federal Student Aid (FASFA) is the only application one must complete to be considered for federal financial aid. The student can request the application from a high school guidance counselor or from a college or university financial aid office. Students can also access and complete the application online by going to http://www.fafsa.us/index.htm. In addition to federal financial aid programs, state agencies for higher education constitute a key piece to the financial aid puzzle. These agencies generally offer a variety of need-based and nonneed-based grants, loans, and work-study packages. Students must be aware that some of the grants are not free; they must be paid back. Additionally, poor performance in college may endanger students' continued eligibility for federal aid. Finally, colleges and universities offer additional financial aid resources, including merit and need-based scholarships, loans, and work-study. Students seeking assistance should contact financial aid offices at the schools to which they are applying. Financial aid offices frequently have prepared packets of information describing any available state, local, and campus-based financial aid as well as information about any forms and applications students must submit to be considered (Gardner, 2000).

QUALITY ACCOMMODATIONS AT POSTSECONDARY LEVELS

According to the Vocational Rehabilitation Act of 1973, and the ADA of 1990, universities and colleges which accept federal funds must provide reasonable accommodations for individuals with disabilities. The key factor in determining whether a person is considered as having a disability is whether the physical or mental impairment results in a substantial limitation of one or more major life activities such as caring for one's self, performing manual tasks, walking, seeing, hearing, speaking, breathing, learning, and working (Rabbe, Silts-Scott, Santa, & Sweringen, 2001). Section 504 and the ADA are the two acts that provide special education services to students with disabilities at the postsecondary level (Madaus, 2005). The ADA was enacted to expand the prohibition against disability discrimination in the private sector and requires that postsecondary institutions make course modifications as long as such modifications do not fundamentally alter the program (ADA, 2004). Under both Section 504 and the ADA, students have the burden to disclose their disability to university officials (see Madaus, 2005) and more specifically, Section 504 prohibits personnel in universities from making inquiries about a student's disability status. Once the university is on notice of the disability, the school must make the appropriate accommodations that are necessary to ensure an opportunity for the student to participate.

Educational Accommodations

In terms of educational accommodations, courts have determined that instructors in higher education need to make reasonable accommodations, which may include implementing learning strategies and innovative teaching techniques (e.g., Nathanson v. Medical College of Pennsylvania, 1991; Wynne v. Tufts University School of Medicine, 1992). About two-thirds of postsecondary students with disabilities receive no accommodations from their schools, primarily because their schools are unaware of their disabilities. In postsecondary schools, students with disabilities are expected to take a greater role in the identification of both their disabilities and the kinds of supports they will receive than they do in secondary schools (Jones, 2002). At the postsecondary level, these students are expected to advocate for themselves (Stodden et al., 2002). To receive accommodations at postsecondary levels, students must voluntarily disclose their disabilities and take the initiative in requesting accommodations. More than half of the postsecondary school students who receive special education services while in secondary school do not consider themselves to have a disability by the time they have transitioned to a postsecondary school. Not surprisingly, then, receipt of accommodations and supports is dramatically less common in postsecondary settings than in high school. Approximately one-third of youth with disabilities in postsecondary schools receive support, accommodations, or other learning aids from their schools (Osgood, Foster, Flanagan, & Ruth, 2005). Receiving appropriate supports and accommodations can be critical to the postsecondary school success and retention of those who are enrolled in postsecondary school programs (Stodden & Dowrick, 2000; Stodden et al., 2002). When discussing accommodations, they can be described as a minimum or a quality accommodation. A minimum accommodation focuses on meeting legal mandates while a quality educational accommodation focuses not only on meeting legal mandates, but also on using best practices to support the learning experience of all students, including those with disabilities (Jones, 2002). See Table 12.1 for a comparison of minimum and quality accommodations.

Table 12.1
Minimum vs. Quality Accommodations

Minimum Accommodation	*Quality Accommodation*
Secondary school student has been invited to participate in Individualized Education Program (IEP) meeting.	Student is invited and encouraged to participate in IEP meeting and then does.
General academic standards are set for all secondary students in the state.	High standards for both academics and career preparation are set for all secondary students in the state.
The student's educational goals are set to achieve outcomes within the current environment.	The student's goals focus upon outcomes to be achieved in both the current and future environments.
Secondary school student (via parents) is regularly informed of student progress.	Self-determination skills are infused into the secondary education curricula and self-determination is actively encouraged in parent/school interactions.
A Statement of Needed Transition Services is included in the student's IEP.	The preparing environment (i.e. secondary school) is gradually molded to fit the receiving environment (i.e. post-secondary school).

Continued on next page

Table 12.1 (continued)

The post-secondary education student must initiate support provision.	Students with disabilities and faculty members are given comprehensive information about, and encouraged to explore, various support options.
In post-secondary school, diverse teaching materials are faculty-specific and require the student to personally advocate for accommodations.	Post-secondary faculty increases their capacity to teach diverse learners, including students with disabilities.

Listening to Students

How do students go about discussing their learning needs with someone like the Director of the Office of Disability Support Services? Role playing the anticipated meeting may help desensitize students toward the actual encounter. If they can first talk about it with their high school resource teacher, then act it out within a safe classroom situation, they will gain confidence in themselves. Gradually, some less positive circumstances should be introduced into the role play to help students to learn how to compensate should they encounter a similar situation in real life. Role reversal also may be helpful (Dexter, 1982). Listening to students is an important educational accommodation.

Making Resources Available

Many resources are available at college and university levels. The Office of Disability Support Services would be a good place to visit to find out what is available. For example, students who have been diagnosed as having learning disabilities are eligible for having their textbooks put on tapes through Recording for the Blind and Dyslexic. Their catalog lists the books currently available on tape according to title and author. If a book is needed that is not on tape, a request can be made to have the book recorded at no charge. It should be noted that the books are taped on special format 15/16 ips, four-track cassettes, with each cassette containing four hours of recorded text. Special player recorders are necessary for use with these cassettes and may be either purchased or loaned. Understanding and using technology can be another key to success. Computers and related technologies are expanding opportunities and increasing instructional access for numerous individuals with disabilities. Students should consider both instructional technology (e.g., computers, tape recorders, or videos used as a means of instruction) and assistive technology (technology used by individuals to compensate for specific disabilities) (Taymans & West, 2001). Providing resources needed by students with disabilities enhances accommodations for them. Colleges and universities must respond to their needs, and they must become advocates for their needs.

CHOOSING A POSTSECONDARY INSTITUTION

Even for students who have struggled academically in high school, postsecondary education may very well be a possibility. Students who wonder whether college is a realistic option can explore summer pre-college courses for high school students who have completed their junior or senior year. Alternatively, students can take a college course the summer before they enroll to get to know the campus, learn how to use the library, and sharpen their study strategies and time management skills (Taymans & West, 2001). Students must determine the characteristics of colleges that will make them happy and support their success. Examples of personal questions to ask include (a) How big is the institution? (b) Will I feel more comfortable in a larger or a smaller college? (c) Will I be happier in an urban or a rural area? (d) Can I meet the academic requirements? Students should start early and talk to teachers, counselors, office of disabilities student services, financial aid offices, and undergraduate support programs at institutions they wish to attend. If students need assistance, then the teacher will need to help them with this process. When investigating colleges, students may also want to consider whether progressive attitudes toward instruction prevail. Colleges that are using instructional techniques and electronic technology in a flexible way can increase students' success. For example, if courses are web-based so lecture notes or videos of presentations are available online and can be viewed multiple times, then students have natural supports built into a course (see Taymans & West, 2001). A student knowing his/her needs and how those can best be met is an important factor when selecting a college. In addition, students with disabilities must (a) look at other factors such as support services offered by colleges, (b) discuss them with college staff, and (c) verify that the services advertised by the college will actually be available to the student. Critical questions may include (a) Is tutoring available? (b) Will extended time be allowed for taking tests? (c) Is someone available to help with taking notes or preparing written work?

Contacting Institutions

Students should call the institution or check for a website on the institution they hope to attend to find our about entrance requirements. If this is something that may be difficult for them, they should be trained to know how to do this through instruction in the transition program by teachers or school counselors. This task should be completed by the first or second year of high school. If the student is unable to meet specific entrance requirements during high school, he/she should attend a local community college to obtain the course requirements he/she is lacking (University of Washington, 2001). If planned appropriately, however, students should have all the needed requirements upon graduation. Students will also probably have to either take the Scholastic Assessment Test (SAT) or the American College Testing (ACT) exam which are offered several times during the school year. Students with disabilities should be aware that they may request accommodations in the testing format or equipment to compensate for their disability. Some of the adaptations which may be requested prior to even applying for acceptance into a college program include (a) extended time, (b) audio cassette edition with regular-type copy, and (c) a reader or a person to record answers. These two tests are also available either untimed or taped and both tests are available in these forms with no additional cost to the student, although special testing times need to be arranged (Cordoni, 1982). It should be noted that accommodations or adaptations in testing procedures or environments must be requested well in advance of the anticipated test date and a student eligibility form must be submitted when requesting accommodations (Rabbe, Silts-Scott, Santa, & Sweringen, 2001). This is crucial as precollege examination (e.g., SAT, PSAT) scores may be important for acceptance into the college of the student's choice.

Institutions of higher learning frequently have divergent opportunities on their campuses for students with disabilities. Postsecondary academies are one-day conference-type events for high school juniors and seniors with a wide range of disabilities. Their parents, teachers, transition specialists, and other high school staff are welcome to attend. Breakout sessions cover specific topics and resemble college classes. In addition, tours of campuses familiarize students with various departments; college recreational programs; the disability services offices; and where to find tutoring, counseling, and advising services (Kato, Nulty, Olszewski, Doolittle, & Flannery, 2006). It is recommended that students visit a campus as early as possible for this orientation so that they can confer personally with an advisor, some of the professors, and the Chairperson of the Special Education Department concerning their special needs. Hopefully, much of this contact is made prior to the admission process; but a second visit would be helpful in most instances (Dexter, 1982). When visiting, students and their parents will want to make sure they also make contact with the Office for Disability Services or Office of Disability Concerns. This office can be contacted to investigate what services are provided to students with disabilities as well as to establish communication with those people who will be involved with the student. The student and the parent can also find out if any further testing is needed. Though programs may vary as to whether the diagnostic testing is done prior to the student's formal acceptance or just after, most institutions conduct an assessment to verify the disability.

Applying for Institutional Admission

When sending an application to a postsecondary institution, students essentially send a portrait of themselves: their grades, coursework, recommendations, personal goals, and abilities. They take time to present a full, positive picture of themselves (University of Washington, 2001). Once admitted, students may request reasonable accommodations to allow them to participate in courses, exams, and other activities. Most colleges and universities have disability support services offices to assist in providing accommodations (Taymans & West, 2001). If possible, the advisor should be visited before classes begin, and some type of regular contract should be maintained throughout the school year. There may be times when a phone call will suffice and other times when an office visit will be necessary. Regardless, an effort should be made to establish a working relationship between the student and his/her advisor (Dexter, 1982). To be successful in college, many individuals with disabilities find it necessary to utilize assistance from campus offices as well as outside resources (University of Washington, 2001).

FINAL THOUGHTS

As the American economy becomes increasingly knowledge based, attaining a postsecondary education becomes more important than ever. The completion of a postsecondary degree has been linked to higher employment rates and higher income in the general population. After high school, students with disabilities need to transition to some other placement/option; and the transition team (along with the student and their parents) should decide what postsecondary option would be best for the student. Based on that decision, the student receives services towards that goal through the transition program. The transition from a high school resource situation to a college campus with no direct services can be devastating for even the brightest student with disabilities. As a result, students must be aware of available services they can access to be as successful as possible. If college is chosen, students and parents should know financial aids might be available to help them with some of the costs of attending college. Students and parents should also realize that it is the obligation of students to identify and document their disability and to request reasonable accommodations. Receiving appropriate supports and accommodations can be critical to the postsecondary school success and retention of those enrolled in postsecondary school programs. Students must determine the characteristics of colleges that will make them happy and support their success and they should call the institution or check for a website to find out about entrance requirements by the first or second year of high school. Regardless of what option is chosen, teachers, parents, and students will need to begin this process early to prepare the student with the knowledge and skills needed to be as successful as possible.

REFERENCES

Adames, S. B. (2000). *An analysis of leadership development among immigrant Latino parents of children with disabilities.* Unpublished master's thesis, University of Illinois, Chicago.

Adams, J. Q., & Welsch, J. R. (1999). *Cultural diversity: Curriculum, classroom, and climate.* Macomb, IL: Illinois Staff and Curriculum Developers Association.

Agran, M., Martin, J. E., & Mithaug, D. E. (1989). Transitional programming: Suggesting an adaptability model. In S. E. Breuning & R. A. Gable (Eds.), *Advances in mental retardation and developmental disabilities* (pp. 179–208). Greenwich, CT: JAI.

Alberto, P. A., Mechling, L., Taber, T. A., & Thompson, J. (1995). Using videotape to communicate with parents of students with severe disabilities. *Teaching Exceptional Children, 27*(3), 18-21.

Americans with Disabilities Act of 1990, PL 101–336, 42 U.S.C. 12101 et seq. (1990).

Anderson, R. J., & Strathe, M. I. (1987). Career education for special needs youth. In G. D. Meers (Ed.), *Handbook of vocational special needs education* (2nd ed., pp. 259–274). Rockville, MD: Aspen.

Arnett, J. J. (2000). Emerging adulthood: A theory of development from the late teens through the twenties. *American Psychologist, 55,* 469–480.

Bailey, D, Jr., Skinner, D., Rodriguez, P., Gut, D., & Correa, V. (1999). Awareness, use, and satisfaction with services for Latino parents of young children with disabilities. *Exceptional Children, 65,* 367–381.

Bakken, J. P. (1998). Powerful yet simple: Being an effective teacher using the daily lesson plan. *Quality in Higher Education, 7*(5), 1–2.

Bakken, J. P., & Aloia, G. F. (1999). Transitioning multicultural learners with exceptionalities. In F. E. Obiakor, J. O. Schwenn, & A.F. Rotatori (Eds.), *Advances in special education: Multicultural education for learners with exceptionalities* (pp. 217–232). Stamford, CT: JAI Press.

Ball, A. L., Garton, B. L., & Dyer, J. E. (2001). The influence of learning communities and 4–H/FFA participation on college of agriculture students' academic performance and retention. *Journal of Agricultural Education, 42,* 54–62.

Basterra, M. del R. (1998, April). *Overcoming structural barriers to promote Latino parental involvement.* Paper presented at the annual meeting of the American Educational Research Association, San Diego, CA.

Bauminger, N. (1990). *Main characteristics of social skills in adolescents with learning disabilities.* Unpublished master's thesis, The Hebrew University of Jerusalem, Israel.

Beirne-Smith, M., Ittenbach, R. F., & Patton, J. R. (1998). *Mental retardation* (5th ed.). Upper Saddle River, NJ: Merrill.

Bennett, C. C. (2003). *Facilitating the job search for special needs clients.* (ERIC Document Reproduction Service No. ED 480 499).

Berry, J. O., & Hardman, M. L., (1998). *Lifespan perspectives on the family and disability.* Needham Heights, MA: Allyn & Bacon.

Biller, E. (1988). *Career decision making for adolescents and young adults with learning disabilities: Theory, research, and practice.* Springfield, IL: Charles C Thomas.

Black, R. S., & Langone, J. (1997). Social awareness and transition to employment for adolescents with mental retardation. *Remedial and Special Education, 18*(5), 214–222.

Blackorby, J., & Wagner, M. (1996). Longitudinal postschool outcomes of youth with disabilities: Findings from the national longitudinal transition study. *Exceptional Children, 62*, 399–413.

Boone, R. S. (1992). Involving culturally diverse parents in transition planning. *Career Development for Exceptional Individuals, 15*(2), 205–221.

Bourland, E. (1996). *Travel training for youth with disabilities.* (ERIC Document Reproduction Service No. ED 399 751).

Bremer, C. D., & Smith, J. (2004). Teaching social skills. *Information Brief: Addressing Trends and Developments in Secondary Education and Transition, 3*(5), 1–5.

Brolin, D. E. (1989). *Life-centered career education: A competency-based approach.* Reston, VA: The Council for Exceptional Children.

Brolin, D. E. (1996). Reflections on the beginning . . . and the future directions! *Career Development for Exceptional Individuals, 19*, 93–100.

Burgstahler, S. (2003). The role of technology in preparing youth with disabilities for postsecondary education and employment. *Journal of Special Education Technology, 18*(4), 7–19.

Callicott, K. J. (2003). Culturally sensitive collaboration within person-centered planning. *Focus on Autism and Other Developmental Disabilities, 18*, 60–69.

Cameto, R., Levine, P., Wagner, M., & Marder, C. (2005). *The emerging independence of youth with disabilities.* (A report from the National Longitudinal Transition Study-2, NLTS2). Menlo Park, CA: SRI International.

Cameto, R., Marder, C., Wagner, M., & Cardoso, D. (2003). *Youth employment.* (A report from the National Longitudinal Transition Study). Menlo Park, CA: SRI International.

Campbell-Whatley, G. D., Algozzine, B., & Obiakor, F. (1997). Using mentoring to improve academic programming for African American male youths with mild disabilities. *The School Counselor, 44*, 362–366.

Campbell-Whatley, G. D., Obiakor, F. E., & Algozzine, B. (1997). Effects of programming on youngsters at risk. *The Journal of At-Risk Issues, 4*(1), 3–9.

Cardon, P. L. (2000). At-risk students and technology education: A qualitative study. *Journal of Technology Studies, 26*, 49–57.

Carey, J. C., Boscardin, M. L., & Fontes, L. (1994). Improving the multicultural effectiveness of your school. In P. Pedersen & J. C. Carey (Eds.), *Multicultural counseling in schools: A practical handbook* (pp. 239–249). Boston: Allyn & Bacon.

Carnevale, A. P., & Desrochers, D. M. (2003). *Standards for what? The economic roots of K-16 reform.* Princeton, NJ: Educational Testing Service.

Carnevale, A. P., & Fry, R. A. (2000). *Crossing the great divide: Can we achieve equity when generation Y goes to college?* Princeton, NJ: Educational Testing Service.

Cartledge, G. (2005). Learning disabilities and social skills: Reflections. *Learning Disability Quarterly, 28,* 179–181.

Cartledge, G., & Milburn, J. F. (1996). *Cultural diversity and social skills instruction: Understanding ethnic and gender differences.* Champaign, IL: Research Press.

Catsambis, S. (2002). Expanding knowledge of parental involvement in children's secondary education: Connections with high school seniors' academic success. *Social Psychology of Education, 5*(2), 149–177.

Cawley, J., Kahn, H., & Tedesco, A. (1989). Vocational education and students with learning disabilities. *Journal of Learning Disabilities, 22,* 630–634.

Chadsey-Rusch, J. (1992). Toward defining and measuring social skills in employment settings. *American Journal on Mental Retardation, 96,* 405–418.

Chadsey-Rusch, J., Karlan, G. M., & Rusch, F. (1984). Competitive employment: Teaching conversation skills to adults who are mentally retarded. *Mental Retardation, 22,* 218–225.

Chadsey-Rusch, J., & O'Reilly, M. F. (1992). Social integration in employment and post-secondary educational settings: Outcomes and process variables. In F.R. Rusch, L. DeStafano, J. Chadsey-Rusch, L. Phelps, & E. Syzmanski (Eds.), *Transition from school to adult life: Models, linkages, and policy* (pp. 245–264). Sycamore, IL: Sycamore.

Chadsey-Rusch, J., Rusch, F., & O'Reilly, M. F. (1991). Transition from school to integrated communities. *Remedial and Special Education, 12,* 1–8.

Chalip, L., Thomas, D. R., & Voyle, J. (1992). Sport, recreation and well-being. In D. R. Thomas & H. Veno (Eds.), *Psychology and social change* (pp. 132–156). Polminton North, New Zealand: Dunmore Press.

Cheek, F. (2003). *Coaching the job seeker with special needs.* (ERIC Document Reproduction Service No. ED 482 758).

Clark, G. M., & Kolstoe, O. P. (1995). *Career development and transition education for adolescents with disabilities* (2nd ed.). Boston: Allyn and Bacon.

Cobb, B., & Hasazi, S. (1987). School aged transition services: Options for adolescents with mild handicaps. *Career Development of Exceptional Individuals, 10,* 15-18.

Cohen M., & Besharov, D. J. (2002). *The role of career and technical education: Implications for the federal government.* (ERIC Document Reproduction Service No. ED 466 939).

Collett-Lingenberg, L. L. (1998). The reality of best practices in transition: A case study. *Exceptional Children, 65,* 67–78.

Combes, B. H., & Durodoye, B. A. (2007). Multicultural special education transition programming. In F. E. Obiakor (Ed.), *Multicultural special education: Culturally responsive teaching* (pp. 206–223). Upper Saddle River, NJ: Merrill.

Cordoni, B. K. (1982). Postsecondary education: Where do we go from here? *Journal of Learning Disabilities, 15,* 265–267.

Cotton, P., Goodall, S., Bauer, J., Klein, J., Covert, S., & Nisbet, J. (1992). *Moving from school to adulthood: The role of circles of support in the transition process.* Durham, NH: The Institute on Disability, University of New Hampshire.

Danley, K. S., & Anthony, W. A. (1987). The choose-get-keep model: Serving severely psychiatrically disabled people. *American Rehabilitation, 13*(4), 6–9, 27–29.

Danseco, E. R. (1997). Parental beliefs on childhood disability: Insights on culture, child development and intervention. *International Journal of Disability, Development, and Education, 44*, 41–51.

Davidson, N. (1994). Cooperative and collaborative learning: An integrative perspective. In J. S. Thousand, R. A. Villa, & A. I. Nevin (Eds.), *Creativity and collaborative learning: A practical guide to empowering students and teachers* (pp. 13–30). Baltimore: Brookes.

De Carvalho, M. E. P. (2001). Family-school interactions: Lessons from personal experience. In M. E. P. de Carvalho (Ed.), *Rethinking family-school relations: A critique of parental involvement in schooling: Sociocultural, political, and historical studies in education* (pp. 29–42). Mahwah, NJ: Erlbaum.

deFur, S. (2003). IEP transition planning-from compliance to quality. *Exceptionality, 11*(2), 115–128.

deFur, S. H., & Patton, J. R. (Eds.)(1999). *Transition and school-based services.* Austin, TX: Pro-Ed.

deFur, S. H., Todd-Allen, M., & Getzel, E. E. (2001). Parent participation in the transition planning process. *Career Development for Exceptional Individuals, 24*(1), 19–36.

DeMario, N. (1992). Skills needed for successful employment: A review of the literature. *RE:view, 24*, 115–122.

Department of Ageing, Disability & Home Care. (2006). *Group homes.* www.dadhc.nsw.gov.au/dadhc/People+with+a+disability/Accomodation.htm.

Dexter, B. L. (1982). Helping learning disabled students prepare for college. *Journal of Learning Disabilities, 15*, 344–346.

Disability Rights Commission. (2006). *Residential services: Marketing and information.* http://www.drc.org.uk/employers_and_service_provider/education/higher_education/residential_services.aspx.

Dukes, L. L., & Shaw, S. F. (1999). Post-secondary disability personnel: Professional standards and staff development. *Journal of Developmental Education, 23*(1), 26–31.

Eckes, S.E., & Ochoa, T. (2005). Students with disabilities: Transitioning from high school to higher education. *American Secondary Education, 33*(3), 6–20.

Education for All Handicapped Children's Act of 1975. (P. L. 94–142). Washington, DC: U.S. Government Printing Office.

Eisenman, L. (2001). Conceptualizing the contribution of career-oriented schooling to self-determination. *Career Development of Exceptional Individuals, 24*(1), 3–6.

Elrod, G. F. (1987). Academic and social skills pre-requisite to success in vocational training. *The Journal of Vocational Special Needs Education, 10*, 17–21.

Emerson, E., Beasley, F., Offord, G., & Mansell, J. (1992). An evaluation of hospital-based specialized staff housing for people with seriously challenging behaviors. *Journal of Intellectual Disability Research, 36*, 291–307.

Englert, C. S., Tarrant, K. L., & Mariage, T. V. (1992). Defining and redefining instructional practice in special education: Perspectives on good teaching. *Teacher Education and Special Education, 15*(2), 62–86.

Evers, R. (1996). The positive force of vocational education: Transition outcomes for youth with learning disabilities. *Journal of Learning Disabilities, 29*, 69–78.

Everson, J. M., & Moon, M. S. (1987). Transition services for young adults with severe disabilities: Defining professional and parental roles and responsibilities. *Journal of the Association for Persons with Severe Handicaps, 12*, 87–95.

Experience-Based Career Education. (1976). *Experience-based career education: Basic procedures manual.* Fort Dodge, IA: Iowa Central Community College.

Farren, C., Gray, J. D., & Kaye, B. (1984). Mentoring: A boon to career development. *Personnel, 61*, 20–24.

Field, S., Hoffman, A., & Spezia, S. (1998). *Self-determination strategies for adolescents in transition.* Austin, TX: Pro-Ed.

Fillmore, L. W. (1986). Teaching bilingual learners. In M. C. Wittrock (Ed.), *Handbook of research on teaching* (3rd ed.) (pp. 648–685). New York: Macmillan.

Fine, M., & Asch, A. (1988). Disability beyond stigma: Social interaction, discrimination, and activism. *Journal of Social Issues, 44*, 3–21.

Flexer, R. W., Simmons, T. J., Luft, P., & Baer, R.M. (2005). *Transition planning for secondary students with disabilities.* Upper Saddle River, NJ: Pearson Education.

Frieden, L., Richards, L., Cole, J., & Bailey, D. (1979). *ILRU source book: A technical assistance manual independent living research utilization project.* Houston, TX: The Institute for Rehabilitation Research.

Fullerton, A., Brannan, S., & Arick, J. (2000). *The impact of camp programs on children with disabilities: Opportunities for independence.* (ERIC Document Reproduction Service No. ED 454 029).

Funk & Wagnalls New International Dictionary of the English Language. (1995). Chicago, IL: World.

Gandolfo, C., & Graham, A. (1998). *ICI tools for inclusion. An examination of teaching a networking strategy to job seekers.* (ERIC Document Reproduction Service No. ED 466 939).

Gardner, D. (2000). *Financial aid for individuals with learning disabilities.* (ERIC Document Reproduction Service No. ED 469 336).

Gardner, D., & Hartman, R. (1997). *Financial aid for students with disabilities.* (ERIC Document Reproduction Service No. ED 407 758).

Gardner, D. C., & Warren, S. A. (1978). *Careers and disabilities: A career education approach.* Stamford, CT: Greylock.

Geenan, S., Powers, L. E., & Lopez-Vasquez, A. (2001). Multicultural aspects of parent involvement in transition planning. *Exceptional Children, 67*, 265–282.

Gerber, P. J., Ginsberg, R., & Reiff, H. B. (1992). Identifying alterable patterns in employment success for highly successful adults with learning disabilities. *Journal of Learning Disabilities, 20*, 43–52.

Goldhammer, K., & Taylor, R. E. (1972). *Career education: Perspective and promise.* Columbus, OH: Merrill.

Goldstein, H., & Morgan, L. (2002). Social interaction and models of friendship development. In H. Goldstein, I. A. Kaczmarek, & K. M. English (Eds.). *Promoting social communication: Children with developmental disabilities from birth to adolescence* (pp. 5–25). Baltimore: Paul H. Brookes.

Goupil, G., Tasse, M. J., Garcin, N., & Dore, C. (2002). Parent and teacher perceptions of individualized transition planning. *British Journal of Special Education, 29*(3), 127–135.

Green, J. E., & Weaver, R. A. (1994). *Tech prep: A strategy for school reform.* Bloomington, IN: Phi Delta Kappa Educational Foundation.

Greene, G. (1996). Empowering culturally and linguistically diverse families in the transition planning process. *Journal for Vocational Special Needs Educators, 19*(1), 26–30.

Greene, G., & Nefsky, P. (1999). Transition for culturally and linguistically diverse youth with disabilities: Closing the gaps. *Multiple Voices, 3*(1), 15–24.

Greenspan, S., & Shoultz, B. (1981). Why mentally retarded adults lose their jobs: Social competence as a factor in work adjustment. *Applied Research in Mental Retardation, 2*, 23–38.

Gresham, F. M., Elliott, S. N., & Black, F. L. (1987). Teacher-rated social skills of mainstreamed mildly handicapped and nonhandicapped children. *School Psychology Review, 16*(1), 78–88.

Gresham, F. M., Sugai, G., & Horner, R. H. (2001). Interpreting outcomes of social skills training for students with high-incidence disabilities. *Exceptional Children, 67*, 331–344.

Grigal, M., Neubert, D. A., Moon, M. S., & Graham, S. (2003). Self-determnation for students with disabilities: Views of parents and teachers. *Exceptional Children, 70*, 97–112.

Gumpel, T. (1994). Social competence and social skills training for persons with mental retardation: An expansion of a behavioral paradigm. *Education and Training in Mental Retardation and Developmental Disabilities, 29*, 194–201.

Hall, J. A., Ford, L. H., Moss, J. W., & Dineen, J. P. (1986). Practice with mentally retarded adults as an adjunct to vocational training. *Social Work, 31*, 125–129.

Halpern A. S. (1992). Transition: Old wine in new bottles. *Exceptional Children, 58*(3), 202–211.

Halpern, A. (1993). Quality of life as a conceptual framework for evaluating transition outcomes. *Exceptional Children, 59*, 486–498.

Halpern, A. S., Yovanoff, R, Doren, B., & Benz, M. R. (1995). Predicting participation in postsecondary education for school leavers with disabilities. *Exceptional Children, 62*, 151–164.

Hanley-Maxwell, C., Pogoloff, S. M., & Whitney-Thomas, J. (1998). Families: The heart of transition. In F. R. Rusch & J. G. Chadsey (Eds.), *Beyond high school: Transition from school to work* (pp. 234–264). Belmont, CA: Wadsworth.

Harner, C., & Heal, L. (1993). The multifaceted lifestyle satisfaction scale (MLSS): Psychometric properties of an interview schedule for assessing personal satisfaction of adults with limited intelligence. *Research in Developmental Disabilities, 14*, 221–236.

Harrington, T. (1982). *Handbook of career planning for students with special needs* (2nd ed.). Austin, TX: Pro-Ed.

Harry, B. (1992). *Cultural diversity, families, and the special education system.* New York: Teachers College Press.

Harry, B., Allen, N., & McLaughlin, M. (1995). Communication versus compliance: African-American parents' involvement in special education. *Exceptional Children, 61*, 364–377.

Harry, B., Rueda, R., & Kalyanpur, M. (1999). Cultural reciprocity in sociocultural perspective: Adapting the normalization principle for family collaboration. *Exceptional Children, 66*, 123–136.

Harry, B., Torguson, C., Katkavich, J., & Guerrero, M. (1993). Crossing social class and cultural barriers in working with families. *Teaching Exceptional Children, 26*(1), 48–51.

Harvey, M. W. (2001). The efficacy of vocational education for students with disabilities concerning post–school employment outcomes: A review of the literature. *Journal of Industrial Teacher Education, 38*, 25–44.

Hasazi, B., & Cobb, S. B. (1987). School-aged transition services: Options for adolescents with mild handicaps. *Career Development for Exceptional Individuals, 10*(1), 15–23.

Hasazi, S. B., Gordon, L. R., & Roe, C. A. (1985). Factors associated with the employment status of handicapped youth exiting high school from 1979 to 1983. *Exceptional Children, 51*, 445–469.

Hatton, C., Emerson, E., Robertson, J., & Henderson, D. (1995). The quality and costs of residential services for adults with multiple disabilities: A comparative evaluation. *Research in Developmental Disabilities, 16*, 439–460.

Heller, T., Markwardt, R., Rowitz, L., & Farber, B. (1994). Adaptation of Hispanic families to a member with mental retardation. *American Journal on Mental Retardation, 99*, 289–300.

Hester, E. J., & Stone, E. (1984). *Utilization of worksite modifications.* Topeka, KS: The Menninger Foundation.

Hill, B., Rotegard, L., & Bruininks, R. (1984). The quality of life of mentally retarded people in residential care. *Social Work, 29*, 275–281.

Hilliard, A. G. (1992). Behavioral style, culture, and teaching and learning. *Journal of Negro Education, 61*, 370–377.

Hosp, J. L., & Reschly, D. J. (2004). Disproportionate representation of minority students in special education academic, demographic, and economic predictors. *Exceptional Children, 70*, 185–199.

Hotchkiss, J. L. (2003). *The labor market experience of workers with disabilities: The ADA and beyond.* Kalamazoo, MI: W.E. Upjohn Institute for Employment Research.

Hutchins, M. P., & Renzaglia, A. (1998). Interviewing family for effective transition to employment. *Teaching Exceptional Children, 30*(4), 72–78.

Hutchinson, N. (1995). *Career counseling of youth with learning disabilities.* Greensboro, NC: ERIC Clearinghouse on Counseling and Student Services. (ERIC Document Reproduction Service No. ED 400 470).

Illinois Assistive Technology Project. (n.d.). *Teens transition to the future.* Retrieved September 1, 2004 from www.iltech.org/rights_passage.htm.

Independent Living Institute. (2006). *Promoting disabled people's self-determination.* www.independentliving.org.

Individuals with Disabilities Education Act Amendments of 1990 (P. L. 104–476). Washington, DC: U.S. Government Printing Office.

Individuals with Disabilities Education Act. (1997) *Individuals with Disabilities Education Act Amendments of 1997. P. L. 105–17,* June 4, 1997 20 U.S.C., 1412. (Formerly titled the Education of the Handicapped Act Amendments of 1990 [P. L. 101–476]), 37–157.

Individuals with Disabilities Education Improvement Act of 2004. (2004). *Public Law 108–446,* HR 1350.

Isaacson, L. E., & Brown, D. (1983). *Career information, career counseling, and career development* (5th ed.). Boston: Allyn and Bacon.

Iso-Ahola, W.E. (1980). *The social psychology of leisure and recreation.* Dubuque, IA: William C. Brown.

Johnson, R. T., & Johnson, D. W. (1994). An overview of cooperative learning. In J. S. Thousand, R. A. Villa, & A. I. Nevin (Eds.), *Creativity and collaborative learning: A practical guide to empowering students and teachers* (pp. 31–44). Baltimore: Paul H. Brookes.

Jones, M. (2002). *Providing a quality accommodated experience in preparation for and during post-secondary school.* (ERIC Document Reproduction Service No. ED 466 064).

Jones, M. (2006). Teaching self-determination: Empowered teachers, empowered students. *Teaching Exceptional Children, 39*(1), 12–17.

Jones, Y. G., & Velez, W. (1997). *Effects of Latino parent involvement on academic achievement.* Paper presented at the annual meeting of the American Educational Research Association, Chicago, IL.

Kagan, S. (1992). *Cooperative learning.* San Juan Capistrano, CA: Resources for Teachers.

Kailes, J. I. (2006). *An orientation to independent living centers.* http://www.jik.com/ilcorien.html.

Kalyanpur, M., & Harry, B. (1999). *Culture in special education: Building reciprocal family-professional relationships.* Baltimore: Paul H. Brooks.

Kalyanpur, M., & Rao, S. S. (1991). Empowering low income black families of handicapped children. *American Journal of Orthopsychiatry, 61,* 523–532.

Kato, M. M., Nulty, B., Olszewski, B. T., Doolittle, J., & Flannery, K. B. (2006). Postsecondary academies. Helping students with disabilities transition to college. *Teaching Exceptional Children, 39*(1), 18–23.

Kaye, S. (1997). *The status of people with disabilities in the United States.* Disability watch. Volcano, CA: Volcano Press.

Kiernan, W. (2000). Where are we now: Perspectives on employment of persons with mental retardation. *Focus on Autism and Other Developmental Disabilities, 15,* 90–96.

Kiernan, W. E., & Schalock, R. L. (1997). *Integrated employment: Current status and future directions.* Washington, DC: American Association on Mental Retardation.

Kiernan, W. E., & Stark, J. A. (Eds.). (1986). *Pathways to employment for adults with developmental disabilities.* Baltimore: Paul H. Brookes.

Kilburn, J., & Critchlow, J. (1998). *Best practices for coordinating transition services: Information for consumers, parents, teachers and other service providers.* (ERIC Document Reproduction Service No. ED 460 466).

Kim-Rupnow, W. S., & Burgstahler, S. (2004). Perceptions of students with disabilities regarding the value of technology-based support activities on postsecondary education and employment. *Journal of Special Education Technology, 19*(2), 43–56.

Kohler, P. D. (1993). Best practices in transition: Substantiated or implied? *Career Development for Exceptional Individuals, 16,* 107–120.

Kohler, P. (1996). Preparing youth with disabilities for future challenges: A taxonomy for transition programming. In P. D. Kohler (Ed.), *Taxonomy for transition programming: Linking research and practice* (pp. 1–62). Champaign, IL: Transition Research Institute, University of Illinois at Champaign-Urbana.

Kohler, P. D., & Field, S. (2003). Transition-focused education: Foundation for the future. *The Journal of Special Education, 37,* 174–183.

Krom, D. M., & Prater, M. A. (1993). IEP goals for intermediate-aged students with mild mental retardation. *Career Development for Exceptional Individuals, 16,* 87–95.

Krumboltz, J. D., & Baker, R. D. (1973). Behavioral counseling for vocational decisions. In H. Borow (Ed.), *Career guidance for a new age* (pp. 235–284). Boston: Houghton-Mifflin.

Larson, C. (1981). *EBCE State of Iowa dissemination model for MD and LD students.* Fort Dodge, IA: Iowa Central Community College.

Leake, D., & Cholymay, M. (2004). Addressing the needs of culturally and linguistically diverse students with disabilities in post secondary education. *Information Brief, 3*(1). Retrieved from www.ncset.org.

Leung, B. P. (1996). Quality assessment practices in a diverse society. *Teaching Exceptional Children, 28,* 42–45.

Linan-Thompson, S., & Jean, R. (1997). Completing the parent participation puzzle: Accepting diversity. *Teaching Exceptional Children, 3,* 46–50.

Lindstrom, L. E., & Benz, M. R. (2002). Phases of career development: Case studies of young women with learning disabilities. *Exceptional Children, 69,* 67–83.

Lord, M. A. (1997). Leisure's role in enhancing social competencies of individuals with developmental disabilities. *Parks and Recreation, 32*(4), 35–40.

Ludi, D.C., & Martin, L. (1995). Choicemaker: A comprehensive self-determination transition program. *Intervention in School and Clinic, 30,* 147–156.

Luft, P., Koch, L. C., Headman, D., & O'Connor, P. (2001). Career and vocational education. In R. W. Flexer, T. J. Simmons, P. Luft, & R. M. Baer (Eds.), *Transition planning for secondary students with disabilities* (pp. 162–196). Upper Saddle River, NJ: Merrill/Prentice Hall.

Lynch, E. W., & Hanson, M. J. (1992). *Developing cross-cultural competence: A guide or working with young children and their families.* Baltimore: Paul H. Brookes.

Lytle, R. K., & Bordin, J. (2001). Enhancing the IEP team: Strategies for parents and professionals. *Teaching Exceptional Children, 33*(5), 40–44.

MacWilliam, L. J. (1977). You can get . . . there---from---here. Travel and community experience for multiply handicapped students. *Teaching Exceptional Children, 9*(2), 49–51.

Madaus, J.W. (2005). Navigating the college transition made: A guide for students with learning disabilities. *Teaching Exceptional Children, 37*(3), 32–37.

Mangan, T. (1992). Promoting integration on the job: Building natural support in the workplace. *What's Working, 1,* p. 5.

Mank, D. (1994). The underachievement of supported employment: A call for reinvestment. *Journal of Disability Policy Studies, 5*(2), 1–24.

Mansell, J. (1995). Staffing and staff performance in services for people with severe or profound learning disability and serious challenging behavior. *Journal of Intellectual Disability Research, 39*, 3–14.

Marland, S. P., Jr. (1971). *Career education now.* Speech presented before annual convention of National Association of Secondary School Principals, Houston, TX.

Martin, J. E., Marshall, L. H., & Maxon, L. L. (1993). Transition policy: Infusing self-determination and self-advocacy into transition programs. *Career Development for Exceptional Individuals, 16*(1), 53–61.

McAfee, J.K., & Greenawalt, C. (2001). IDEA, the courts, and the law of transition. *Preventing School Failure, 45*, 102–107.

McAvoy, L. (2001). Outdoors for everyone: Opportunities that include people with disabilities. *Parks and Recreation, 36*(8), 24, 26, 28, 30, 32–33, 35–36.

McNair, J., & Rusch, F. R. (1990). *Parent involvement in transition programs.* Urbana, IL: University of Illinois (ERIC Document Reproduction Service No. ED 331 229).

Meers, G. C. (1987). An introduction to vocational special needs education. In G. D. Meers (Ed.), *Handbook of vocational special needs education* (2nd ed., pp. 3–28). Rockville, MD: Aspen.

Michaels, C. A., Thaler, R., Zwerlein, R., Gioglio, M., & Apostoli, B. (1988). *How to succeed in college: Keys to success for students with learning disabilities.* Albertson, NY: Human Resources Center.

Miner, C.A., & Bates, P. E. (1997). The effect of person centered planning activities on the IEP/transition planning process. *Education and Training in Mental Retardation and Developmental Disabilities, 32*, 105–112.

Misra, A. (1992). Generation of social skills through self-monitoring by adults with mild mental retardation. *Exceptional Children, 58*, 495–507.

Mithaug, D. E., Horiuchi, C. N., & Fanning, P. N. (1985). A report on the Colorado statewide follow-up survey of special education students. *Exceptional Children, 51*, 397–404.

Mithaug, D. E., Martin, J. E., & Agran, M. (1987). Adaptability instruction: The goal of transitional programming. *Exceptional Children, 53*, 500–505.

Modell, S., Rider, R., & Menchetti, B. (197). An exploration of the influence of educational placement on the community recreation and leisure patterns of children with developmental disabilities. *Perceptual and Motor Skills, 85*, 695–704.

Modell, S. J., & Valdez, L. A. (2002). Beyond bowling: transition planning for students with disabilities. *Teaching Exceptional Children, 34*(6), 46–52.

Moery, K. (1993). *After high school . . . ? Building on today for tomorrow. Designing and implementing a community-based, family-sentered transistion planning project. A manual for professionals, arents, and youth with disabilities.* Chicago: Office of Special Education and Rehabilitative Service.

Moon, S., Goodall, P., Barcus, M., & Brooke, V. (1986). *The supported work model of competitive employment for citizens with severe handicaps: A guide for job trainers.* Richmond, VA: Rehabilitation Research and Training Center, Virginia Commonwealth University.

Morgan, R. L., Gerity, B. P., & Ellerd, D. A. (2000). Using video and CD-ROM technology in a job preference inventory for youth with severe disabilities. *Journal of Special Education Technology, 15*(3), 25–33.

Morningstar, M. E., Kleinhammer-Tramill, P. J., & Lattin, D. L. (1999). Using successful models of student-centered transition planning and services for adolescents with disabilities. *Focus on Exceptional Children, 31*(9), 1–19.

Morningstar, M., & Lattin, D. (1996). *Student involvement in transition planning* (Training Module). Lawrence, KS: University of Kansas, Department of Special Education.

Morningstar, M. E., Turnbull, A. P., & Turnbull, H. R. (1996). What do students with disabilities tell us about the importance of family involvement in the transition from school to adult life? *Exceptional Children, 62,* 249–260.

Mull, C. A., & Sitlington, P. L. (2003). The role of technology in the transition to postsecondary education of students with disabilities: A review of the literature. *The Journal of Special Education, 37*(1), 26–32.

Nathanson v. Medical College of Pennsylvania, 926 F.2d 1368 (3rd Cir. 1991).

National Center on Secondary Education and Transition. (2003). *A national leadership summit on improving results for youth: State priorities and needs for assistance.* Retrieved July 19, 2004, from http://www.ncset.org/summit03/NCSETSummit03findings.pdf.

National Council on Disability. (2000). *Transition and post-school outcomes for youth with disabilities: Closing the gaps to post-secondary education and employment.* Washington, DC: Author.

National Organization on Disability. (1998). *The 1998 N.O.D.J Harris survey of Americans with disabilities.* New York: Louis Harris & Associates.

NATRI. (2004). *Assistive technology continuum.* Retrieved September 8, 2004 from natri.uky.edu/resources/fundamentals/defined.html#continuum.

Navarrete, L. A., & White, W. J. (1994). School to community transition planning: Factors to consider when working with culturally diverse students and families in rural settings. *Rural Special Education Quarterly, 13,* 51–56.

Nelson, C. M. (1988). Social skills training handicapped students. *Teaching Exceptional Children, 20*(4), 19–23.

Neubert, D.A., & Moon, M. S. (2000). How a transition profile helps students prepare for life in the community. *Teaching Exceptional Children, 33*(2), 20–25.

New Mexico Health Care Association (2002). *Intermediate care facilities for the mentally retarded.* http://www.nmhca.org/pages/choose_icfmr.htm.

Newman, L. (2005). *Postsecondary education participation of youth with disabilities.* (A report from the National Longitudinal Transition Study-2, NLTS2). Menlo Park, CA: SRI International.

Nicolau, S., & Ramos, C. L. (1990). *Together is better: Building strong partnerships between schools and Hispanic parents.* New York: Hispanic Policy Development Project.

Nisbet, J., & Hagner, D. (1988). Natural supports in the workplace: A reexamination of supported employment. *Journal of the Association for Persons with Severe Handicaps, 13,* 260–267.

NLTS. (1993). *What makes a difference? Influences on postschool outcomes of youth with disabilities.* (The Third Comprehensive Report of the National Longitudinal

Transition Study of Special Education Students). Menlo Park, CA: SRI International.

NLTS. (2005). *After high school: A first look at the postschool experiences of youth with disabilities.* (A report from the National Longitudinal Transition Study-2, NLTS2, Executive Summary). Menlo Park, CA: SRI International.

Nochajski, S. M., Oddo, C., & Beaver, K. (1999). Technology and transition: Tools for success. *Technology and Disability, 11*, 93–101.

Obiakor, F. E. (2004). Impact of changing demographics on public education for culturally diverse learners with behavior problem: Implications for teacher preparation. In L. M. Bullock & R. A. Gable (Eds.), *Quality personnel preparation in emotional/behavorial disorders: Current perspectives and future directions* (pp. 51–63). Denton, TX: University of North Texas, Institute for Behavioral and Learning Differences.

Obiakor, F. E., Algozzine, B., Thurlow, M., Gwalla-Ogisi, N., Enwefa, S., Enwefa, R., & McIntosh, A. (2002). *Addressing the issue of disproportionate representation: Identification and assessment of culturally diverse students with emotional or behavioral disorders.* Arlington, VA: Council for Exceptional Children.

Obiakor, F. E., & Utley, C. A. (1997). Rethinking preservice preparation for teachers in the learning disabilities field: Workable multicultural strategies. *Learning Disabilities Research & Practice, 12*, 100–106.

O'Connor, C., & Fernandez, S. D. (2006). Race, class, and disproportionality: Reevaluating the relationship between poverty and special education placement. *Educational Researcher, 35*(6), 6–11.

Office for Civil Rights, U.S. Department of Education. (2004). *Students with disabilities preparing for postsecondary education: Know your rights and responsibilities,* from http://www.ed.gov/about/offices/list/ocr/transition.html#reproduction.

Ohio Valley Educational Cooperative. (1996, September). Project Trails: Student Enhancement Project. Retrieved February 14, 2005 from www.ed.uiuc.edu/sped/tri/TPWorksheet.htm.

O'Reilly, M. F., Lancioni, G., & Kierans, I. (2000). Teaching leisure social skills to adults with moderate mental retardation: An analysis of acquisition, generalization, and maintenance, *Education and Training in Mental Retardation and Developmental Disabilities, 35*, 250–258.

Osgood, D. W., Foster, E. M., Flanagan, C., & Ruth, G. (2005). Introduction: Why focus on the transition to adulthood for vulnerable populations? In W. Osgood, M. Foster, C. Flanagan, and G. Ruth (Eds.), *On your own without a net: The transition to adulthood for vulnerable populations* (pp. 1–26). Chicago, IL: University of Chicago Press.

PACER Center. (1998). *Supported employment: An introduction.* Minneapolis, MN: Author.

Parents Let's Unite For Kids (PLUK). (2004). *Family guide to assistive technology.* Retrieved September 8, 2004 from www.pluk.org/AT1.html#2.

Park, H. S., & Gaylord-Ross, R. (1989). A problem-solving approach to social skills training in employment settings with mentally retarded youth. *Journal of Applied Behavior Analysis, 22*, 373–380.

Parker, J. G., & Asher, S. R. (1987). Peer acceptance and later personal adjustment: Are low-accepted children "at risk?" *Psychological Bulletin, 102*, 357–389.

Parrish, L. H., & Kok, M. R. (1985). *Procedures handbook for special needs work-study coordinators.* Rockville, MD: Aspen.

Patrikakou, E. N. (2004). *Adolescence: Are parents relevant to high school students' achievement.* Chicago, IL: FINE Network, Harvard Family Research Project.

Patton, J. R., & Browder, P. M. (1988). Transitions into the future. In B. L. Ludlow, A. P. Turnbull, & R. Luckasson (Eds.), *Transitions to adult life for people with mental retardation: Principles and practices* (pp. 293–312). Baltimore: Paul H. Brookes.

Phillips, P. (1990). A self-advocacy plan for high school students with learning disabilities: A comparative case study analysis of students', teachers', and parents' perceptions of program effects. *Journal of Learning Disabilities, 23*, 466–471.

Pierangelo, R., & Giuliani, G. A. (2004). *Transition services in special education: A practical approach.* Boston: Pearson Education.

Pruitt, P., Wandry, D., & Hollums, D. (1998). Listen to us! Parents speak out about their interactions with special educators. *Preventing School Failure, 42*(4), 161–166.

Quinn, M. M., Jannasch-Pennell, A., & Rutherford, R. B. (1995). Using peers as social skills training agents for students with antisocial behavior: A cooperative learning approach. *Preventing School Failure, 39*(4), 26–31.

Rabbe, B., Silts-Scott, S., Santa M. K., & Sweringen, T. (2001). *Beyond high school: Exploring vocational education and other options for students with disabilities and exploring military options for students with disabilities.* (ERIC Document Reproduction Service No. ED469 459).

Rehabilitation Act of 1973, P.L. 93–112, 29 U.S.C 701 *et seq.*

Reimer-Reiss, M. L., & Wacker, R. R. (2000). Factors associated with assistive technology discontinuance among individuals with disabilities. *Journal of Rehabilitation, 66*(3), 44–50.

Repetto, J. B., & Correa, V. I. (1996). Expanding views on transition. *Exceptional Children, 62*, 551–563.

Riley, R. W. (1995). Reflections on goals 2000. *Teachers College Record, 96*, 380–388.

Ross, J. E. (2001). *Water-based outdoor recreation and persons with disabilities.* (ERIC Document Reproduction Service No. ED 463 940).

Rusch, F., & Menchetti, B. (1981). Increasing compliant work behaviors in a non-sheltered work setting. *Mental Retardation, 19*, 107–111.

Rusch, F. R., & Phelps, L. A. (1987). Secondary special education and transition from school to work: A national priority. *Exceptional Children, 53*, 487–492.

Rusch, F. R., Szymanski, E., & Chadsey-Rusch, J. (1992). The emerging field of transition services. In F. Rusch, L. DeStefano, J. Chadsey-Rusch, L. A. Phelps, & E. Szymanski (Eds.), *Transition from school to adult life: Models, linkages, and policy* (pp. 5–17). Sycamore, IL: Sycamore Press.

Russell, R. (1996). *Pastimes: The context of contemporary leisure.* Madison, WI: Brown and Benchmark.

Sabornie, E. J., & Beard, G. H. (1990). Teaching social skills to students with mild handicaps. *Teaching Exceptional Children, 23*(1), 35–38.

Salembier, G., & Furney, K. S. (1997). Facilitating participation: Parents' perceptions of their involvement in the IEP/transition planning process. *Career Development for Exceptional Individuals, 20*(1), 29–42.

Sanchez, S. Y. (1999). Learning from the stories of culturally and linguistically diverse families and communities. *Remedial and Special Education, 20*, 351–359.

Sandefur, G. D., Martin, M., Eggerling-Boeck, J., Mannon, S. E., & Meier, A. M. (2001). An overview of racial and ethnic demographic trends. In N. J. Smelser, W. J. Wilson, & F. Mitchell (Eds.), *America becoming: Racial trends and their consequences* (pp. 40–102). Washington, DC: National Academy Press.

Sands, D., & Kozleski, E. (1994). Quality of life differences between adults with and without disabilities. *Education and Training in Mental Retardation and Developmental Disabilities, 29*, 90–101.

Santos, S. L., & Santos, R. A. (1984). *Bilingual special education: Issues in bilingual special education* (pp. 27–39). Paper presented at the Bilingual Special Education Conference, Denton, TX.

Sarkees-Wircenski, M., & Scott, J. L. (1995). *Vocational special needs.* Homewood, IL: American Technical Publishers.

Sarkees-Wircenski, M., & Wircenski, J. (1994). Transition planning: Developing a career portfolio for students with disabilities. *Career Development of Exceptional Individuals, 17*, 203–214.

Sauerburger, D. (2005). Street crossings: Analyzing risks, developing strategies, and making decisions. *Journal of Visual Impairments and Blindness, 99*, 659–663.

Schalock, R. L., Wolzen, B., Ross, I., Elliot, B., Werbel, G., & Peterson, K. (1986). Postsecondary community placement of handicapped students: A five-year follow-up. *Learning Disability Quarterly, 9*, 295–303.

Schleien, S. J., Tipton R. M., & Green, F. P. (1997). *Community recreation and people with disabilities: Strategies for inclusion* (2nd ed.). Baltimore: Paul H. Brookes.

Schloss, P.J., Alper, S., & Jayne, D. (1994). Self-determination for persons with disabilities; Choice, risk, and dignity. *Exceptional Children, 60*, 215–255.

School-to-Work Opportunities Act of 1994. (P. L. 103–239). Washington, DC: U.S. Government Printing Office.

Schumaker, J. B., & Hazel, J. B. (1984). Social skills assessment and training for the leaning disabled: Who's on first and what's on second? Part II. *Journal of Learning Disabilities, 17*, 492–499.

Shapiro, E. S., & Lentz, F. (1991). Vocational-technical programs: Follow-up of students with learning disabilities. *Exceptional Children, 58*, 47–49.

Shectman, Z. (1993). Group counseling in school in order to improve social skills among students with adaptation problems. *The Educational Counselor, 3*(1), 47–67.

Simon, M. (2001). Beyond broken promises: Reflections on eliminating barriers to the success of minority youth with disabilities. *JASH, 26*, 200–203.

Sitlington, P.A. (1996). Transition to living: The neglected component of transition programming for individuals with learning disabilities. *Journal of Learning Disabilities, 29*, 31–39.

Sitlington, P. L., Clark, G. M., & Kolstoe, O. P. (2000). *Transition education & services for adolescents with disabilities* (3rd ed.). Boston: Allyn and Bacon.

Sitlington, P. L., & Frank, A. R. (1993). Dropouts with learning disabilities: What happens to them as young adults? *Learning Disabilities Research & Practice, 8*, 244–252.

Smith, R. W. (1985). Barriers are more than architectural. *Parks and Recreation, 20* (10), 58–62.

Smith, M. S., & Scoll, B. W. (1995). The Clinton human capital agenda. *Teachers College Record, 96*, 389–404.

Stodden, R. A., Conway, M. A., & Chang, K. B. T. (2003). Findings from the study of transition, technology and postsecondary supports for youth with disabilities: Implications for secondary school educators. *Journal of Special Education Technology, 18*(4), 29–43.

Stodden, R. A., & Dowrick, P. (2000). The present and future of postsecondary education for adults with disabilities. *IMPACT, 13*(1), 4–5.

Stodden, R. A., Jones, M. A., & Chang, K. B. T. (2002). *Services, supports, and accommodations for individuals with disabilities: An analysis across secondary education, post-secondary education and employment.* Retrieved November 22, 2006, from http://www.ncset.hawaii.edu/publications/pdf/services_supports.pdf.

Strain P. S., & Odom, S. L. (1986). Peer social initiations: Effective intervention for social skills development of exceptional children. *Exceptional Children, 52,* 543–551.

Strand, J., & Kreiner, J. (2001). Recreation and leisure in the community. In R. W. Flexer, T. J. Simmons, P. Luft, & R. M. Baer (Eds.), *Transition planning for secondary students with disabilities* (pp. 474–497). Upper Saddle River, NJ: Merrill.

Stumbo, N. J. (1995). Social skills instruction through commercially available resources. *Therapeutic Recreation Journal, 29*(1), 30–55.

Sue, D. W., Bingham, R. P., Porche-Burke, L., & Vasquez, M. (1999). The diversification of psychology: A multicultural revolution. *American Psychologist, 54,* 1061–1069.

Sue, D. W., & Sue, D. (1999). *Counseling the culturally different: Theory and practice* (3rd ed.). New York: Wiley.

Sugai, G., & Lewis, T. (2004). Social skills instruction in the classroom. In C. Darch & E. J. Kameenui (Eds.). *Instructional classroom management: A proactive approach to behavior* (2nd ed., pp. 152–172). Upper Saddle River, NJ: Merrill.

Symanski, E. M., & Hershenson, D. B. (1998). Career development of people with disabilities: An ecological model. In E. M. Symanski & R. M. Parker (Eds.), *Rehabilitation counseling: Basics and beyond* (3rd ed., pp. 327–378). Austin, TX: Pro-Ed.

Szymanski, E.M., Hewitt, G.J., Watson, E.A., & Swett, E.A. (1999). Faculty and instructor perception of disability support services and student communication. *Career Development of Exceptional Individuals, 22*(1), 117–128.

Tashie, C., Malloy, J. M., & Lichtenstein, S. J. (1999). Transition or graduation? Supporting all students to plan for the future. In C. J. Jorgensen (Ed.), *Restructuring high schools for all students: Taking inclusion to the next level* (pp. 233–260). Baltimore: Paul H. Brookes.

Taylor, B., McGilloway, S., & Donnelly, M. (2004). Preparing young adults with disability for employment. *Health and Social Care in the Community, 12,* 93–101.

Taymans, J. M., & West, L. (2001). *Selecting a college for students with learning disablities of attention deficit hyperactivity disorder(ADHD).* (ERIC Document Reproduction Service No. ED 461 957).

Temelini, D., & Fesko, S. (1996). *Shared responsibility: Job search practices from the consumer and staff perspective.* Boston: Institute for Community Inclusion (UAP), Children's Hospital.

The Workforce Investment Act of 1998, Public Law 105–220 (29 U.S.C. 718).

Thompson, J. R., Fulk, B. M., & Piercy, S. W. (2000). Do individualized transition plans match the post-school projections of student with learning disabilities and their parents? *Career Development for Exceptional Individuals, 23*(1), 3–25.

Thorp, E. K. (1997). Increasing opportunities for partnership with culturally and linguistically diverse families. *Intervention in School and Clinic, 32,* 261–269.

Trainor, A. A. (2005). Self-determination perceptions and behaviors of diverse students with LD during the transition planning process. *Journal of Learning Disabilities, 38*(3), 233–249.

Trupin, L., Sebesta, D. S., Yelin, E., & LaPlante, M. P. (1997). Trends in labor force participation among persons with disabilities, 1983–1994. In *Disability statistics report* (Vol. 10). Washington, DC: U.S. Department of Education, National Institute on Disability and Rehabilitation Research.

Turnbull, A. P., & Turnbull, H. R. (2000). *Families, professionals, and exceptionalities: Collaboration for empowerment.* Englewood Cliffs, NJ: Prentice-Hall.

Turnbull, A. P., & Winton, P. J. (1984). Parent involvement policy and practice: Current research and implications for families of young, severely handicapped children. In J. Blacker (Ed.), *Severely handicapped young children and their families* (pp. 377–397). New York: Academic Press.

University of Washington. (2001). *College: You can do it! How students with disabilities can prepare for college.* (ERIC Document Reproduction Service No. ED 477 408).

U.S. Department of Education. (1994). *Sixteenth annual report to Congress on the implementation of the Individuals with Disabilities Education Act.* Washington, DC: Office of Special Education Programs.

Vocational Rehabilitation Act of 1973, PL 93–112, 29 U.S.C., 701 et seq.

Voltz, D. L. (1994). Developing collaborative parent-teacher relationships with culturally diverse parents. *Intervention in School and Clinic, 29,* 288–291.

Voltz, D. L. (1998). Cultural diversity and special education teacher preparation: Critical issues confronting the field. *Teacher Education and Special Education, 21,* 63–70.

Wagner, M., Blackorby, J., Cameto, R., & Newman, L. (1993). *What makes a difference? Influences on postschool outcomes of youth with disabilities.* Menlo Park, CA: SRI International.

Wagner, M., Newman, L., Cameto, R., Garza, N., & Levine, P. (2005). *After high school: A first look at the postschool experiences of youth with disabilities.* (A report from the National Longitudinal Transition Study-2, NLTS2). Menlo Park, CA: SRI International.

Ward, L., Mallett, R., Heslop, P., & Simons, K. (2003). Transition planning: How well does it work for young people with learning disabilities and their families? *British Journal of Special Education, 30*(3), 132–137.

Ward, M. J. (1988). The many facets of self-determination. *National Information Center for Children & Youth with Handicaps: Transition Summary, 5,* 2–3.

Ward, M. J., & Halloran, W. D. (1993). Transition issues for the 1990s. *OSERS News in Print: Transitions, 6*(1), 4–5.

Warger, C., & Burnette, J. (2000). *Planning student-directed transitions to adult life.* Reston, VA: ERIC Clearinghouse on Disabilities and Gifted Education. (ERIC Document Reproduction Service No. ED 439 577).

Wehman, P. (1992). *Life beyond the classroom: Transition strategies for young people with disabilities.* Baltimore: Paul H. Brookes.

Wehman, P. (1996). *Life beyond the classroom: Transition strategies for young people with disabilities.* Baltimore: Paul H. Brookes.

Wehman, P., & Kregel, J. (1995). At the crossroads: Supported employment ten years later. *Journal of the Association for Persons with Severe Disabilities, 20,* 286–299.

Wehmeyer, M. L. (1992) Self-determination and the education of students with mental retardation. *Education & Training in Mental Retardation, 27,* 302–314.

Wehmeyer, M. L. (1995). A career education approach: Self-determination for youth with mild cognitive disabilities. *Intervention in School and Clinic, 30,* 157–163.

Wehmeyer, M. L. (1998) Student involvement in transition-planning and transition-program implementation. In F. Rusch & J. G. Chadsey (Eds.), *Beyond high school: Transition from school to work* (pp. 206–233). Belmont, CA: Wadsworth.

Wehmeyer, M. L., Agran, M., & Hughes, C. (2000). A national survey of teachers' promotion of self-determination and student-directed learning. *Journal of Special Education, 34,* 58–68.

Wehmeyer, M. L., & Sands, D. J. (1998). *Making it happen: Student involving in education planning, decision making, and instruction.* Baltimore: Paul. H. Brookes.

Wehmeyer, M. L., & Schwartz, M. (1997). Self-determination and positive adult outcomes: A follow-up study of youth with mental retardation or learning disabilities. *Exceptional Children, 63,* 245–255.

Weiss, B. D., & Coyne, C. (1997). Communicating with patients who cannot read. *The New England Journal of Medicine, 337,* 272–274.

Wielandt, T., & Scherer, M. (2004). Reducing AT abandonment: Proposed principles for AT selection and recommendation. Retrieved October 11, 2004 from e-bility.com/articles/at_selection.shtml.

Wilder, L. K., Jackson, A. P., & Smith, T. B. (2001). Secondary transition of multicultural learners: Lessons from the Navajo Native American experience. *Preventing School Failure, 45* (3), 119–124.

Will, M. (1984). *OSERS programming for the transition of youth with disabilities: Bridges from school to working life.* Washington, DC: U.S. Department of Education.

Wilson, K. E. (1998). Centers for independent living in support of transition. *Focus On Autism and Other Developmental Disabilities, 13,* 246–252.

Wolanin, T. R., & Steele, P. E. (2004). *Higher education opportunities for students with disabilities.* Washington, DC: The Institute for Higher Education Policy.

Wolfe, P.S., Boone, R. S., & Blanchett, W. J. (1998). Regular and special educators' perception of transition competencies. *Career Development for Exceptional Individuals, 21*(1), 87.

Wynne v. Tufts University School of Medicine, 976 F.2d 791 (1st Cir. 1992).

Yelin, E., & Trupin, L. (1997, November). *Successful labor market transitions for persons with disabilities: Factors affecting the probability of entering and maintaining employment.* Paper prepared for the conference on Employment Post the Americans with Disabilities Act, Washington, DC.

Zabala, J. (1996). *SETTing the stage for success: Building success through effective selection and use of assistive technology systems.* Paper presented at the Southeast Augmentative Communication Conference, Birmingham, AL.

Zabala, J. (2002, March). A brief introduction to the SETT Framework. Retrieved October 11, 2004 from www.joyzabala.com.

Zhang, D., & Benz, M. R. (2006). Enhancing self-determination of culturally diverse students with disabilities: Current status and future directions. *Focus on Exceptional Children, 38*(9), 1–12.

Zins, J..E., Elias, M. J., Weissberg, R. P., Greenberg, M. T., Haynes, N. M., & Frey, K. S. (1998). Enhancing learning through social and emotional education. *Think: The Journal of Creative and Critical Thinking, 9*, 18–20.

NAME INDEX

SUBJECT INDEX

A

Ability Hub, 53
ABLEDATA, 53
Accommodations, 162–165
Adult education, 17, 155–156
Advocacy services, 146
African American students, 30–31
Alliance for Technology Access (ATA), 54
American College Testing (ACT) exam, 166
Americans with Disabilities Act (ADA, 1990)
  accommodations, 161–162
  demographics, 82
  employment, 11
  job interview, 93
  support services, 157
  vocational/technical education, 154
Answers 4 Families, 79
Appalachia Education Laboratory Model, 15
Apprenticeships, 90, 156
Assis-TECH, 53
Assistive technology (AT)
  choosing most appropriate, 46–52
  definitions, 41–43
  providing, 43–46
    services by school district, 44–46
  web resources, 52–57
    information and resources, 54–55
    products, 53–54
    research, 56–57
    training, 55–56
Assistivetech.net, 54
AT Network, 54–55

B

"Bridge" model, 14–15

C

Career academies, 89
Career development
  academies, 89
  apprenticeships, 90, 156
  appropriate job, choosing, 85–86
  and colleges, 153–157
  educational programs, 108–109
    tech-prep, 89
    vocational-technical, 89
  job search methods, 91–94
    interview, 93–94
    networking, 91–92
    resume, 93
  job skills, necessary, 83–85
  parental involvement, 156–157
  placement services, 124
  postsecondary experiences, 154–156
  professional, 87–88
  stages, 16–17
  trade and technical schools, 89–90
  work-study programs, 88
  see also Employment; Vocational programs
Career education
  comprehensive model (CCEM), 16–17
  movement, 14
  and technical (CTE), 108–109
CCEM (Comprehensive career education model), 16–17
Centers for independent living (CIL) (*see* Independent living)
Citizenship (and independent living), 141–142
CLD (*see* Diversity)
Closing the Gap, Inc., 55
Colleges and universities
  admission, applying for, 167–168

195

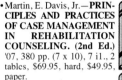
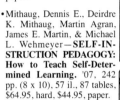

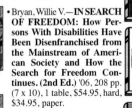
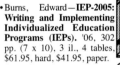
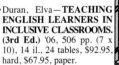

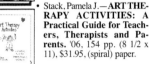
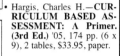

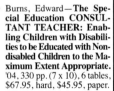

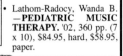